GROWING
BOLD

HOW TO OVERCOME FEAR, BUILD
CONFIDENCE, AND LOVE THE LIFE YOU LIVE

GROWING

BOLD

PATRICIA C. BROOKS

Growing Bold: How to Overcome Fear, Build Confidence, and Love the Life You Live may be purchased for educational or business use.
For information contact
Perpignan Press, P.O. Box 28425, Richmond, VA 23228
info@perpignanpress.com

Centering Exercises by Sharlene Cooke
Author Photo by Kim Brundage Photography
Cover and Book design by Vanessa Mendozzi Design
Images used under license "Shutterstock.com"

ISBN 978-0-9977599-0-7

First Edition

To my mom and dad,
who still guide me.

CONTENTS

Rivers and Dreams   1

Chapter 1 - The Bold Life   11

Chapter 2 - Kick-Start Your Dreams   31

Chapter 3 - Lift the Veil   49

Chapter 4 - Shed the Past   63

Chapter 5 - Run with the Stars   89

Chapter 6 - Steer with Purpose   109

Appendixes   135
Appendix 1 - The Three Catalysts   137
Appendix 2 - Exploring, Mapping, Claiming   139
Appendix 3 - Values   141
Appendix 4 - Centering   143

Bibliography   149
Acknowledgments   153

INTRODUCTION
RIVERS AND DREAMS

"Life is a river of passing events. Swift is its current." When I was in my twenties, my mother read me this, the senior-class quote from her 1954 high school yearbook. Just out of college, I'd moved back home and was showing her pictures of all the friends I'd made and would miss.

She smiled with me as I recounted my college escapades. She spoke of her own friends and memories. She headed for the hall closet and dug out her own yearbooks. I can still see her thumbing through the pages to the twelfth grade, pointing out a young girl she claimed was herself. She laughed at my teasing. Catching sight of the quotation, she paused before reading it aloud. It clearly held deep meaning. After that day, as if seeing the words again had reminded her, she repeated them when friends' grandchildren were born, or when someone died.

Though those words did not reach me then, they haunt me now. I lost my mother and father relatively young, losses that recalled to me those words, and that awakened me to the reality that life ends, even for those who were my world. A year ago, my high-school sweetheart succumbed to cancer at 49. Such losses teach us how short life really is, and how early some of us meet the reaper.

Our turn, too, will come. Our chance to be happy, to accomplish things, and to make a difference in this world will also end. This thought doesn't depress me, though, it energizes me, stirring my passion to help others find happiness and meaning in their lives. Time is short, that's true: too short not to love the life you live.

I don't fear dying. I used to fear it, because the thought of spending my life unhappy and of doing things that held little meaning for me used to make me feel I'd wasted precious time. I used to feel that the time I had to make my mark and to affect others positively was running out.

Those feelings moved me to change my ways, changes that revealed to me, and have revealed since to my clients, that when people find their purpose, when they work passionately and joyfully toward achieving it, they light up inside. I did. I know everyone can. That's why I'm writing this now.

Do you love your life? I can honestly say that I do, a statement that continues to amaze me because not too long ago, this was how I *wanted* to feel but wasn't convinced I ever could or would. I say it now. I feel it now. I want you to see how I got here. I want you to feel this way, too.

This book is for you if you're tired of hiding and playing small, bored with your life, discontent with the status quo. It's for you if you want to live boldly, with meaning and purpose. It's for you if you don't want to die with your song unsung, your book unwritten, your dance undanced. It's for you if you want life to offer prospects and possibilities. If you want to say with conviction, "I love my life!"

Growing Bold recounts my own journey, the time-honored pilgrimage from fear, doubt, and conformity to courage, hope, and individuality—a spiritual journey, certainly, honored in every world religion, but also a voyage of discovery, of milestones and insights that can change your life in the here and now as valuably and meaningfully as they've changed mine.

The experiences and life lessons that helped me cultivate faith, desire, and open-mindedness, leading me to where I am today, living a wonderful, purpose-filled life, can do the same for you. Of course, describing my personal journey, while it may add flavor to this discussion, can't substitute for yours. You alone can find and follow the path to your own bold life.

That's why I've included activities and expeditions that will make this book yours. They're designed to help you 1) understand what's truly important to you; 2) know yourself better and accept

3

yourself as you are right now; 3) identify thoughts and beliefs holding you back; 4) move beyond the familiar, and even the comfortable, and toward the life of your dreams.

Journaling activities, an excellent way of writing to yourself and uncovering your most essential feelings, dreams, and wishes, will clear your mind and heal some of life's bumps and wounds. Writing for ourselves alone shakes things inside of us loose and starts us growing in new directions. Resolve to keep a journal or notebook by your side as you progress through this book. Not only will you develop the habit of putting your reactions into words, you'll capture your responses to the activities, responses that will yield insights into your inner world.

———

I entered my hotel room and flung myself across the bed in satisfied exhaustion. The late-May sun slipped past the horizon, touching everything with an eerie, dusky light. I lay quietly, playing over in my mind a day spent exploring. I drifted along to the music of accordions, to the enticing smell of hot crêpes, and the vivid memory of a smiling man in a beret making them. Fields of vineyards and sheep flashed past, quaint little villages built before America was a thought, as I started to drowse. As if falling, I caught myself, jolted awake and into reality, the reality that all this was really happening. That I was here, in Lyon, France, and that two days before, I'd been in Toulouse. I wasn't dreaming. Instead, I'd made one of my dreams real.

I'd spent seven days in France and had seven days left to explore, practice my French, and move past the old boundaries of what I'd thought possible for myself. Lying there, breathing French air and watching French daylight shimmer across the wall, I thought, *Coming here all alone and traveling to four different cities by train is pretty daring. You would never have thought about this, much less actually done it, even a year ago. What's happening?* I puzzled over that, but the answer came swiftly: *You are growing bold.*

How did I get there? And how did I get here, to this place where I'm so very comfortable in my skin, where I like who I am? How can I now take chances I would never have taken ten years, or five years, or even three years ago, experiencing unknown, welcome, exciting, and even daring new challenges? How did I embrace a life in which playing it safe was no longer the first option, choosing instead to feel truly fulfilled?

As I look at myself today, and at the things I undertake, I often give them a quick second glance. Did I just speak that profound thought so clearly and unhesitatingly? Did I just get on a plane from the United States to France and ramble through a foreign country all alone? Did I just give a presentation to a roomful of strangers about myself and my journey, without fear, and with no preparation except the experiences I've chosen for myself? Yes, yes, and yes.

Now, in my forty-ninth year, I'm able to speak up at work, despite the risk of being fired, with little hesitation and no fear. I can see off promising suitors when I realize they're incompatible, not dogged by the fear, or the risk, of being along again, or indefinitely. I can travel internationally, navigating language barriers and transportation systems, while fairly at ease and thoroughly enjoying myself. These actions might not seem remarkable, but they are. For the painfully shy child I was, for the young adult desperate to fit in, they were unimaginable.

Now, quite often, I stand back and smile to myself at the things I go after. The old alarm bells, clanging "What the hell are you doing?" go off in my head unnoticed. These are the signs of my freedom, these are the ways I'm fully experiencing my life. Living with less fear. Pursuing what I'm drawn to, someone stronger and bolder than I was in the past—not only in youth, but even relatively recently. How did this happen? How did I arrive at this boldness? How did I, an insecure, introverted young adult, change into the woman who meets the world today, and enjoys those meetings?

Life itself made some of the changes, but my own efforts to reflect, analyze, and learn from life—efforts I want to help you, too, to make—were the real catalysts for my courage and calmness. The new perceptions I reached not only increased my faith, they stirred a burning desire to learn and grow. Inward reflection led to personal development, painful, and joyful, lessons moved me on.

The beginning of this process, the first moment of truth and difficulty, came when I held to, and examined my values and convictions after my boss asked me to do something that did not sit right. My assignment was to dig up dirt about a director of the company so that management could boot him off the board.

"Collect information that builds a case for termination," the boss said. The conversation felt slimy.

The request was out of bounds. I couldn't agree to character assassination, or to trafficking in gossip, and I certainly couldn't agree to be the underhanded means of reaching such a shady corporate goal. If I couldn't, and didn't, my job was at stake— the good salary, the excellent benefits, the career success, and of course, the life I'd made for myself because of those things.

I tossed and turned all night. In the cold early light of the next day, I wrote out why this assignment wasn't part of my job description. Later that morning, the boss and I met. The moment we sat down, I went off my careful, self-protective script and said, "I won't go on this witch hunt."

Surprised by my forceful resistance, the boss backpedaled, saying I shouldn't construe the request as an investigation. In the end, I prepared a report on the director's projects, something which was part of my job, but I did not furnish the negative or scurrilous information requested.

My refusal meant a demotion. I also lost my office, getting reassigned to a cube just outside the malodorous men's room. I knew when I made my decision that it was career suicide with that organization, but I had to live with myself. Integrity, once breached, is hard to repair.

Weeks later I left that full-time permanent position for a temporary contract job. I had no regrets. I had found my own voice. I realized that my values deserved support. I realized absolutely that the first person to support them had to be me, despite the consequences. That event was the gateway into courage. Financially, I'd lost a great deal. But morally, I'd gained so much more.

That understanding surprised me, and that incident sent me on a different path. Both spurred me to examine past crossroads I'd reached, and earlier choices I'd made. As I proceeded along this new path, these turning points in my life looked different, too. Seeing them differently allowed me to consider many more possible choices, and many more possible actions, not only in the past but in the present and the future: seeing things differently freed me to *do* things differently.

These crucial changes in perspective and attitude let me experience my life with more joy and lightness, with less sadness and stress. Now that I looked at my life more clearly, I saw that the pain of staying the same had become unbearable. It was obvious that I had to find out who I was, assess the deeds I'd done—the bad as well as the good—and really learn what I wanted from my life. "Insanity," as the bumper sticker says, "is doing the same thing over and over again but expecting different results." I stopped that doing, and that expecting.

Shifting perspective was one catalyst that changed my life's chemistry and caused me to Grow Bold. The next was finding faith in myself. The third was harnessing desire. These three helped me move forward. They increased my confidence, cleared my mind, stimulated my compassion, and unlocked a depth of authenticity, creativity, self-discipline, and inner peace that allows me to stand for what's real and to live with a purpose.

And what about you? *Something* drew you to this book, and to these ideas. Are you ambitious and successful, or maybe outwardly so, but you still feel a bit hollow, a bit empty? Do you have a vague idea about changing your life without knowing what to change, where to start, or if you should even indulge in such an outrageous fantasy? Or do you have a detailed plan collecting dust in a drawer because you doubt your ability to carry it through?

However you would describe yourself, it's clear that you're weary of your current life situation. You may even be ready to change and expand in daring ways. Ready, but something holds you back. Keep reading.

You'll find yourself here. You'll find that you know how and what will help you on your way. Your active and honest participation in reading this book, and especially doing the activities, can bring you deeper understanding and self-respect, clearer values, a better sense of what's important to you.

You yourself can and will identify what holds you back from the life you want. You yourself will learn ways to change the limiting beliefs and negative patterns of thought that keep you fearful and stuck—the attitudes that make what used to be your comfort zone increasingly uncomfortable.

This book will help you develop self-awareness and self-discipline. Along the way, I hope you will also find inspiration—possibly in my stories, but definitely in yours, those you recount as you complete the activities. They will reveal that you already have the strength and courage to take those next steps. They will reveal your own sources of faith in yourself, a confidence that will sustain you in adversity.

Please continue to read with an open mind. Please be completely honest with yourself as you move through the activities. The more of yourself you put into this process, the more of your stories and of your life, the more clearly you will see what drew you to *Growing Bold*: your life asks your help. Your work with these pages will be your answer.

CHAPTER 1
THE BOLD LIFE

When I told Alex, my ex-husband, that I was writing this book, he said, "Yes, living boldly definitely describes the course you've followed during the last several years."

"On the other hand," he added, "You've always gone after what you want." His assessment was accurate, but he was remembering someone I'd call ambitious, rather than bold. That person certainly had ambition and drive, but she answered to others' standards and steered her course by others' stars.

This person talking to you now, whose life calls her to write this book, has developed something deeper and more lasting than those externally-focused qualities: a certain kind of courage laced with keen intuition. This allows me to go after what I truly want in life with greater confidence and inner faith.

I can work toward what I want with far less fear and far more certainty, but without the extra stress of depending on the final result, or others' judgments, to make me feel whole or happy.

The process itself is the goal.

The ambitious go-getter Alex married and the person I am today resemble each other outwardly, as he said. But inwardly they differ radically. The ambitious go-getter went after things she thought were right for her based on others' ideas. She believed that the paths others took to happiness, or the things they thought she should aspire to, were the right ones.

Even if those paths and aspirations didn't feel quite right, I sought happiness there. I trusted others' ideas more than my own intuition. Today, though, I've discovered my own principles. These, especially my needs for inner peace, for deep connections, for integrity, and for self-mastery, have lit my way. I learned to honor my instincts. I came to understand who I am, and what's really important. Now I see what I truly want and need, and I understand how to secure those wants and needs calmly and confidently.

That crisis at work sparked a succession of achievements. For the first time ever, I negotiated my salary. I facilitated, and with authority, work sessions on subjects new to me, reaching insights that shaped the customer experience. Most importantly, I stopped looking outside myself for approval and contentment. Daunting setbacks and serious losses brought me to that point.

Now, back at a company I'd run from a few years earlier, I fought self-doubt. It felt like repeating after flunking in school. Besides, I was a second-class citizen, with a green badge to let me into the building, not the blue one for full-time employees. Green badge holders were unworthy of health benefits and the other perks for those with blue badges. I felt isolated, the odd woman out.

Besides all that, I was in the middle of an unfriendly divorce. To comfort myself, I ate. I wasn't thin at that point, and I gained even more. It soon became clear that this job wouldn't use my talents, though whether this was because I was a contractor or a black woman, I could not tell. The dissatisfaction and uncertainty added more self-doubt and desolation. Darkening tides of confusion and distress rose, bringing with them bleak bouts of depression. "What is wrong with me?" I asked myself.

Nevertheless, I did appreciate and value being in an environment where I didn't have to sell my soul to survive. This grounded me. Nightly conversations with my mother, who had become a good counsel and wise friend, showed things in a new light and gave me strength.

From my gradually acquired understanding that "this, too, shall pass," arose a resilience I hadn't known before, and the faith that I would inevitably discover, in due time, the necessary lesson. Age brought insight into the unlikely perfection of the things unfolding in my life. Being able to be true to myself, absorbing the wisdom my mother shared, and having faith that my life's experiences were exactly right for me fed my effort to live more boldly.

Each success bolstered my confidence, each setback clarified what was important. Success and failure alike helped me believe in my good judgment and capability, and whetted my appetite for further challenges. The three catalysts—**shifting perspective**, **setting meaningful goals**, and **building self-confidence**— are interrelated and synergistic: time and energy put into any one of them nurtures and strengthens the others. Their power freed me from the neediness and grim determined striving that once darkened my journey. Instead, life came to flow effortlessly, light and pleasant as recreation. Recreation is what it is: my own re-creation of how to be, and how to live.

I now seek challenge as part of my daily life. I don't take the path of least resistance any more, even when I can. When I needed a website, I built it myself. I wanted to learn how. Over a long holiday weekend, I set out to build one, carefully following a two-hour YouTube video. Watching it, and mastering each step, took the whole three days. At the end, I was bleary-eyed and eager to escape the computer, but so satisfied. I'd created a custom website that looked professional.

More recently, I received a project at work that could have been an easy check-the-box exercise. I dug deeper into the project's purpose, asking the sponsor probing questions that needed deeper—and more useful—answers. We worked through the information, reaching a vision of what we needed that satisfied my desire to work on something substantive and the company's need to reduce costs. What began as a simple process-improvement project grew into a full-blown cost-containment effort that can potentially save tens of thousands of dollars.

Finding and answering challenges like these has taught me

new skills, increased my confidence, and strengthened my voice. Going beyond the apparent limits expanded my grasp of what's possible and encouraged me to challenge other boundaries and discover more opportunities. My desire to do more, to use my abilities, will help me find necessary avenues that would otherwise remain hidden.

You might look at the things I undertake and say to yourself, "Why do that? It's too hard. It takes too much time and effort." A few years ago, I would have agreed, but now the idea of living a routine, ordinary life without learning and growing seems like condemning myself to a drab, dreary prison.

"Life is a river of passing events. Swift is its current"—I could not accept the thought that life's swift current could sweep me away, that I could leave this life without having given it my all, and without receiving life's gifts in return. I must make the most of this life now that I know I can, and especially now that I've seen the excitement that my path and my progress sparks in others, friends as well as clients: when they dream, when they understand that they, too, can live a bold life, their insights and energy confirm and inspire my own.

Having outlined what growing bold means to me, I want to look at what it means for you, in this book and in your life. To grow bold means you'll become self-aware. You'll pursue possibilities that were once *im*possibilities. You'll stay true to your values. You'll trust your intuition to navigate life's new prospects confidently and to choose those most suitable for your own unique journey. You'll create a vision, make plans, and take action that turns dreams into realities. And, in the process of growing bold, you will feel and project a confidence unimaginable before and experience a zest for life that is freeing, energizing, and irresistible.

SEEK THE GOAL

Living this bold life requires thoughtful application of three new approaches to yourself and your existence. The first, which is in some ways the hardest, is to **change your mindset**: to move away from skepticism or outright disbelief about what is possible for you to experience, have, or be. These negative viewpoints arise from a limited view of the world around you and your place in it. The challenge is to move toward a broader view that focuses on solutions and possibilities.

The second, linked to and arising from the first, is increased **confidence** that you can achieve your goals. The third, intimately connected to and also nourishing the others, is an intense desire sparked by having a **meaningful goal**.

The shift from skepticism will lead you right into determining a goal that is truly your own. That goal can be as small as pursuing a hobby that lifts your spirits during a less than satisfying work life, or figuring out your own personal fashion style and rocking it, or the goal can be as broad and overarching as a life-purpose statement made up of smaller goals on which you can focus and take action.

Make sure the goal, small or large, is something you are excited about achieving, something specific, and something measurable.

Define your target explicitly; this awakens an intense desire to accomplish it, a desire that moves you to achieve your goal, and moves you as well into the bolder life you want to live. That desire is a transformative force; heed it and tend to it.

Because you're reading this, you probably already have your own ideas about what living a bold life means. You may have even pondered all that comes with living this different way and asked yourself some of the questions: How will you overcome the fear that arises when you step into uncharted territory? How will you deal with the challenges of personal growth, and especially with the mixed emotions surrounding transition and change? How will you release your old reality and embrace a new one? Or maybe you sense that you'll know what your bold life looks and feels like when you're finally living it.

In any case, the first step is defining, clearly and specifically, what your bold life means to you. This is your starting point. From here, you'll make decisions and move forward, specify smaller goals to work on that build confidence, and reach further clarity that will expand on or modify your vision as you go.

Maybe you've already experienced "I wish I could do that" syndrome. You find in yourself strong admiration and appreciation for the path on which someone else embarks. You feel excitement and interest when another reaches a goal, and you wish you had the courage to do bold things, too. Your feelings in these situations suggest that you, like so many, may be living your own dreams through others.

I, too, have encountered wonderful people who live through me. They stand on the sidelines, sincerely rooting for my success. The goals I set and the challenges I seek fascinate them—which makes it so clear that what I'm doing or attempting isn't normal but *is* desirable. When I reset my attitudes and came to live more boldly, I reached those new goals, goals that proved my path had changed.

Going to France alone, happily volunteering to speak publicly, and becoming a published author were *my* goals for living boldly. I fulfilled *my* definition of myself and based goals on *my* desires, experiences, and beliefs. These are simply examples, snapshots of the process and its power.

These snapshots, and this book, are here to help you find *your* definition of yourself, *your* goals, and *your* path. Your bold life will and should include very different goals based on your desires, experiences, and beliefs.

If such goals feel bold to you, if they excite you, and even make you feel a bit anxious or afraid to take the next step, you're on your way! Listen to your own feelings: if you saw someone else doing those things, seeking those goals, would you admire that person's strength and courage? Would you maybe even feel a tad bit jealous? Those, for you, define bold living.

Self-discovery is at the heart of this process. Centering, reflecting, and recording are its simple yet powerful tools. Begin by centering yourself physically, mentally, and emotionally, moving into your own depths and opening yourself to discovery.

Once you center yourself, reflecting and recording bring you awareness and confidence. "Know thyself," Socrates urged his countrymen centuries ago. Twenty-first-century humans, perhaps even more than the ancient Greeks, must contend with obstacles and distractions to reach such knowledge.

Inquiring of yourself, as I will help you do in this book, and writing down the thoughts and feelings that occur to you in an attentive and nonjudgmental way, reveal your deepest desires and your most essential intuitions.

I call this mirror work: a comprehensive look at yourself to assess what's working and what's not. This mirror doesn't reflect wrinkles, scars, clothes or hair. It shouldn't foster shame, blame, regret, or punishment. It is internal, a clear-eyed, penetrating examination of the role your thoughts, feelings and actions play in your present reality and circumstances.

This introspection is your first great achievement, because it brings self-awareness. It moves your growth in new directions and helps you accept and befriend yourself. Introspection uncovers what suits you and what doesn't, and tells you why. The self-awareness it entails brings confidence in your own judgment, letting you say yes or no with conviction when opportunities present themselves.

Introspection also uncovers your past actions, including some arising from the shadow side of your personality. "Beware of your dark side," says a voice I now hear clearly—the voice of Space

Ace, a 1980s video game that Tim, my high-school sweetheart, played constantly.

Back then, I threw temper tantrums when I didn't get what I wanted. At fifteen, for example, two friends and I tried to get into an R-rated movie without an adult. The ticket agent, of course, kept us out. While I pouted and stewed throughout the half-hour walk home, my friends laughed and joked, planning other things to do instead of seeing the movie.

As I look back on this, a memory still so vivid, I cringe. I question that young girl I was. But I must also forgive her youth and self-involvement, the parts of herself at that moment that narrowed her perspective. Older and wiser now, I can see into rejection or apparent injustices and move past those shadow behaviors that trap me in negative feelings and on to Plan B or even Plan C.

This shadow side is a complex psychological concept, but I use it here to refer to characteristics of ourselves that we tamp down and hide, because we consider them, or have been taught to consider them, negative. We all have this side. It's what makes us human. Living boldly means that we continue to examine ourselves and our perspectives, continue to see and accept—again, without shame or blame—those concealed qualities as part of knowing ourselves.

Some years ago, an employee spilled ketchup on the slate floor during lunch at the company cafeteria and simply walked away. Sitting nearby, and appalled at this stranger's carelessness, I called my court into session: *What a slob! Would he leave ketchup on his own floor? People are so rude!* As I prepared to hand down the death penalty, another coworker skidded on the ketchup and crashed onto the hard floor.

Now the judge turned her attention to me. I was part of the problem, a party to the accident. I could have wiped up the spill myself. I could have told the cafeteria staff. Instead, I focused on myself, congratulating myself on how much better I was because I would have cleaned up after myself. Instead of feeling compassion, or even doing something to help, I stayed high and prideful, letting someone else fall.

Later that evening, still feeling guilty, I looked into my behavior in my journal, writing down everything, including my feelings and observations, trying to learn why I'd responded as I had. Examining the incident was difficult, but trying to see what truth about myself it held brought me a shocking understanding.

A long-held need to feel superior, tied somehow to a sense of being inferior as the only minority child in kindergarten, drove my perspective on the ketchup-spiller, as well as my judgmental response. That childhood insecurity, carried in the shadows for so long, not only meant I had to be right; it meant I had to believe myself better than others.

This brittle protection was no security blanket; it could cause someone to get hurt. Clinging to it could hurt me. That moment of insight was sobering. My judgment and inaction were shameful, but looking into those shadow-side responses lit a truth about my nature, changing my perspective forever.

More recently, I looked after my mother as she battled lung

cancer. During one of her stays in the hospital or nursing home, she'd contracted *Clostridium dificile colitis*, a deadly and disgusting diarrhea. After she came home and went into hospice care, she couldn't get the medicine she'd received for it, because her insurance wouldn't pay. Her pain, and the condition's unpleasantness, were unspeakable. She couldn't keep up her strength unless she ate and drank, but she couldn't drink the nourishing Boost shakes she'd grown to love, either, without severe bouts of diarrhea. I *had* to get her the medicine; I had to push hard. Being her advocate now meant keeping after this issue to the point of rudeness. I couldn't fail my mom. I spent hours on the phone, talking to the insurance company, the nursing home, and the pharmacies, demanding they make an exception.

My emotions ran high because it was clear she was close to death. She'd come home to die. Although I don't have kids, when she arrived, it felt as if I were bringing an infant home for the first time. I wanted to make everything perfect for her, a perfection that included getting her that medicine.

I was beside myself. I wasn't proud of my demanding and peremptory manner, and I was deeply disappointed that I couldn't do this one thing for her in her dying days when she had done so much for me. As the days passed and she got closer to the end, I realized the folly of my excitement, but I also realized that I'd seen my mother advocate similarly for my grandmother and stepfather.

I wanted to do as she did, and to reciprocate her kindnesses and sacrifices. My behavior made sense. But I realized, too, that what was now happening put my efforts into perspective. My mother was dying; she would be gone soon. That was what was real. The medicine would alleviate some discomfort, but nothing now could cure or save her.

I accepted my behavior and grew from it, hoping that those I'd been so unpleasant to would understand. Examining the real meaning of this conflict helped me look beyond it to what was about to happen, and helped me come to terms with that. All that I'd done during my lifetime for my mother, especially in her last years, *was* enough. She already felt that way. Not getting that prescription wouldn't change her view of me, or her love for me. A few days before she died, she confirmed this, when she said, "I'm so lucky to have you as my daughter. What would I do without you?" When we parted, we were both at peace.

Your inner thoughts, feelings, and perceptions represent the reality you perceive at any given time, and, of course, affect your responses to events. It follows, then, that the way you responded in the past was the only way possible. That response was therefore correct, although thinking about it may make you uncomfortable.

Discomfort and even regret at uncovering this shadow side is normal, indeed healthy, for it shows that you have moved past the limited awareness that caused the unpleasant, uncomfortable responses. Facing those responses, and those unpleasant feelings directly, helps you become more self-aware. Looking honestly in the mirror frees you from mere regret, helping you discover better ways to respond going forward, ways more in line with your true self.

Painful though they may seem at first, try to move right into such moments of reckoning. They are milestones on your path to self-awareness. If you can look into them now and understand why they feel so painful, wrong, or ill-judged, you'll find that those past actions are guideposts to responding more authentically and less negatively in the future.

Passing over, dismissing, or ignoring them deprives you of self-knowledge and hampers your personal growth. To live boldly means to live from your core—from your heart. You must, therefore, examine and assess, not just forgiving your flaws but understanding them, so that you can move past them.

If you can be truly open and honest, you are more likely to discover your treasure—what is most important to you, and what you want to achieve in your life. Unflinching mirror work helps uncover and dispel internal obstacles to reaching your goals, freeing you to experience the fulfillment, joy, and contentment of living a life you only imagined.

So find yourself a big, spacious notebook. Find a safe, private place to center yourself, to reflect, and to record your thoughts and feelings as you move through *Growing Bold*. Give yourself room, taking as many pages as you need. And give yourself time, writing out your answers as fully as you can. Find, as well, a safe, private place to keep your notebook. Unless you choose to share them, your responses to this book are for your eyes only.

Think yourself into the situations and your answers so that you can be as specific and detailed as possible. If you notice yourself holding back or being guarded as you respond, ask yourself why. Then write about that. If you still feel constrained or unwilling, your answers to these further questions can guide you:

- Who or what causes you to quash past feelings, thoughts, and actions?
- What purpose does silencing those, or not writing about them superficially, serve?
- Do the people or beliefs that make you want to pass over an action or behavior serve your goal of developing the courage and confidence to do what makes you happiest?

Perhaps particular incidents or actions are still so hot for you emotionally that you can't write about them now. In that case, let your words rest in the notebook, take a few minutes, then return. Ask yourself how you want to proceed, and write about that. Awareness doesn't proceed on a lockstep schedule, or sometimes even sequentially. The choice, always, is yours.

The vital thing is to get those thoughts and feelings out of your head and onto the page. When they are there, out in the world, you will see them more clearly. Writing out your responses clears the decks, draining years of bottled-up thoughts and feelings from your mind and making them visible and accessible. Meanwhile, bringing forth all those accumulated and unresolved thoughts and feelings leaves room for new thoughts, ideas, and feelings to flow in, and for seeing yourself and your life in a different, clearer, light.

DISCOVERING YOUR BOLD LIFE

<u>CENTERING</u>

- Close your eyes, belonging to yourself without distraction.
- Find a comfortable position.
- Inhale through your nose for a count of 3; exhale through your nose for a count of 6.
- Take a few breaths in this way, and focus on relaxing your body.
- Attend to your breathing, noticing your shoulders loosening as you exhale.
- Inhale, bringing in the brisk cool air of pure light: this is life force.
- Exhale, sending out the gray heavy cloud of tension.
- Focus on your breathing; notice yourself opening with each breath.
- Let your whole body ease and loosen as you consciously offer it peace:
  - Feel your shoulders relax
  - Feel your arms relax
  - Feel your torso relax
  - Feel your legs relax
  - Feel your feet relax
- In this calm stillness, be with yourself.
- Breathe in energy; breathe out anxiety.
- Breathe in stillness; breathe out fear.
- Continue breathing in this way for as long as you'd like, allow the wave of relaxation to suffuse your entire body.
- When you feel ready, take one last deep breath.
- As you exhale, slowly open your eyes.

- You are ready.

EXPLORING

1. Assume that you have all the necessary resources (time, money, talent, support, etc.) to realize the goal you want to achieve most in life.

   What goal would you set and start working toward immediately? Write out that goal in as much detail as necessary.

2. What would success in attaining this goal look like? Consider these questions in writing your answer:
   - How will you determine if you have been successful?
   - What must success include?
   - What factors must be present for you to feel satisfied with your accomplishment?

3. Describe your life once you've reached this goal, giving your vision in as much detail as possible.
   - How will achieving your goal make a difference, in your life or that of others?
   - Detail the difference it will make.
   - How will reaching this goal affect your life and the lives of your family members?
   - Consider all aspects of your life, including finances, health, career, personal development, family, relationships, fun and enjoyment, spirituality, etc.

4. Why is reaching this goal so important to you? To help you specify and explore the details, consider these questions:
    - What will be different in your life after you accomplish this?
    - How will you feel after doing so?
    - What will you be able to do once you achieve your goal?

5. Look at your answers to Question 4 and drill down just a bit further. Consider and explain why what you feel, and what you'll be able to do after reaching your goal, is so important to you.
    - Why is feeling the way you will feel after achievement important?
    - Why is experiencing your life as you will be able to experience it after attaining your goal so vital to you?

6. Once more, imagine that no barriers exist to your success and that you've worked hard and steadily toward your goal. That day has arrived: you've now reached your goal. Close your eyes and picture what your life looks like after achieving your goal. Paint as detailed a picture as possible. Write out your vision.

Questions to consider:
    - What are you doing (in all aspects of your life) at the moment pictured?
    - Who are you doing it with?
    - Where are you living? How much income are you earning?
    - What are you doing for fun?
    - What difference are you making in the world every day?
    - What do you feel, see, smell, hear, and know?

7. When you've finished describing your new life, read the description aloud.

8. Write down how considering and recording all these things felt to you. What thoughts and emotions did these questions and answers stir? Jot those down.

We will revisit your vision in a later chapter. Tying back to your feelings and senses now, after recording your responses, offers insight. Revisiting those feeling and senses will offer more as we continue.

RETURNING

- Breathe in for a count of 3 and out for a count of 6.
- Close your eyes.
- Envision your success one more time.
- Feel the excitement.
- Bask in the feeling of accomplishment.
- Delight in your confidence.
- Give thanks for your strength.
- When you feel ready, take one more deep breath.
- Hold it briefly at the top, feeling your power.
- Exhale slowly as you open your eyes.
- Congratulate yourself!

CHAPTER 2
KICK-START YOUR DREAMS

The explorations you did in the last chapter got you dreaming again, didn't they? You revisited what you want most from life. Sometimes we get so stuck in daily routines, going to work and paying the bills, helping others and trying to get our to-do lists finished, that dust and cobwebs bury our dreams, hiding them even from us. Reinhabiting your dreams and inner passions puts you in touch with the first catalyst to boldness: **setting meaningful goals** that stoke desire. The other two, which you will also explore in this chapter, are **changing perspectives**, and **increasing self-confidence**.

This process, living boldly and living from the center of yourself, from your own truth, requires honesty and persistence. And it can be painful.

QUESTION THE PLAN

Have you ever done something based on a master plan that seemed perfectly sound and plausible at the time, one you absolutely knew would work out, but in the end it didn't? Have you found yourself miserable, wondering how the plan could have turned out so badly? Have you examined your life because you had to, and learned during that examination not only that the plan doesn't fit, but that it never could have fit *you*?

Believe me, I know. It's always difficult, and often painful, to question the plan. Here's what that moment felt like for me:

> *Damn it! How did things end up this way, heading for divorce? My plan was perfect, yet we are arguing. We sleep apart, and we dislike and resent each other. I am so angry, I feel compelled to scream—like a madwoman. My feelings are so dark that my heart feels burnt.*

I'd concocted and lived out my plan, a plan based on the flawed, fear-filled perspective I had at that time. But the marriage had become a nightmare. I had to face that. To face it meant to feel the pain, the loss, the sorrow, and the responsibility—the flaws in my understanding of life, of love, of him, and of myself. Meanwhile, I learned that my father had been sick and now was terminally ill.

The beginning and the end of the marriage were actually different sides of the same coin, the same life. On one side was my belief that I needed a husband for financial reasons, as a means to escape a bad job.

I cringe as I write this, but it's the truth: I liked the man I married well enough, but it was *like*, not love, and *like* isn't something I should have married for. I was 37, and *I* knew best. If we married, I'd get his health insurance, which meant I could leave a job I hated and pursue my very successful side job in sales full time.

Marriage was the perfect escape. I see the folly of it all now, but as I was considering this and taking steps to make it happen, it made perfect sense. The result of following the plan was a marriage that harmed and poisoned us both.

On the other side of that coin, as things went downhill, was my readjusted perception, which included the painful knowledge that I had used him, and used the idea of marriage, for selfish aims, and the realization that I did not, in fact, need a husband in order to have a good life.

Long after I could get any financial benefit from my husband, I stayed married. Even after I faced my wrong in using him that way, I still kept to the plan, trying to right my mistake and maintain the marriage by being a loving, caring, and loyal wife.

Concerned that he wasn't saving, I asked him about that one day. "That's why I have you," he answered. That let the cat out of the bag: although I had used him during the first six months of our marriage, he expected to use me for financial security. This insight was an even more painful revelation about myself.

Now it was undeniable that I, too, had played a role, and lived untruthfully. Even after I realized my bad motives, and long after the marriage brought any financial, let alone emotional, benefit, I chose to stay married: I couldn't discard the plan. I put in six years of loyalty, and of needing to be right, pretending I *was* right, to avoid admitting failure.

I'd spent six years hiding from my own part in creating a marriage that now was clearly doomed. Its doom forced me to look into the plan, and into the decisions I'd made to achieve the plan. When I questioned the plan, my perspective changed, a change that helped me think more clearly and act differently.

The revelation that he was choosing to stay married for money and not love, and that he was unwilling to do what we'd both have to do to fix a broken relationship, increased my desire to leave him, a desire that caused me to make a very different plan. I became determined to dissolve the marriage within a year.

Before that year was up, my father died. Daddy's death, however, confronted me with another reality: life itself is only temporary. Daddy's death made it clear how carelessly I was living mine in a misbegotten relationship. Meanwhile, the marriage deteriorated further.

Facing these truths honestly, especially those unpalatable ones about myself, paradoxically tapped a hidden wellspring of confidence. The energy I spent hiding the truth from myself now became the strength to act. That strength, that desire, blossomed from seeing things differently—even though changing my perspective was painful—and helped me act in accord with my new perceptions. Only after revisiting these painful events could I act, because only the truths they showed made my next move clear.

"The truth shall set you free," the Bible says, and that's been my experience. Facing my own truth showed me I could create and sustain change. It sparked a burning desire to experience life differently, regardless of inconvenience, difficulties, or even obstacles. In the light of this self-awareness, the overblown threats I'd always feared shrank to hindrances I could surmount or go around: I told my husband to leave the house, and I filed for divorce.

Desire was not only my strength, it was my guide, leading me to take the steps that helped me grow and become my own best friend. Desire's vigor also hushed the voices of fear and doubt so that I could experience peace, a peace that remains part of my life today.

Despite the stress and pain of severing a marriage, my newly acquired respect for the fleeting quality of life kept me working to see things through, fueling the steps I'd started. Steps I'd taken based on confidence and inner strength I found in my relationship with my father during his dying days.

My last image of my father was through tears, as he struggled to lift his emaciated left arm during a physical therapy session. During the last six days of his life, he dwindled to skin and bone. I watched as he struggled to do this simple thing, a strong man still, unwilling to languish in bed, even in his deathbed. And he raised that arm. The image is seared in my memory, a reminder of who I am and where I come from. My father was a strong man, even in his last days. And I am his child.

In the months and years since, I've often called back this last image of my father when I faced a challenge or felt unsure of my own strength.

Remembering it caused me to stand against that injustice at work, despite retaliation and demotion.

Remembering it moved me past physical exhaustion during karate trials so that I could earn six belts—now I'm at purple, with only brown and black left.

Remembering it gave me confidence that I could handle my ex's venomous tirades during divorce proceedings, my shame and embarrassment over how the marriage started and how it went, and my loneliness in its aftermath.

When I invoke my father's strength, especially that last sight of it, I reach into my own. Doing so invariably increases my confidence in my abilities—the third catalyst to Growing Bold. Besides shifting your perspective, and setting an intention that will awaken your strong desire, you must cultivate one thing more to live boldly: increased self-confidence. This is belief in yourself, an unshakeable conviction that you can navigate your plan for change. My father holds the key to that for me. The key for you may be a person, too, or it may be an occasion, experience, or achievement.

Before my father died, I'd wanted to end my marriage, but my desire to do so became a *burning* desire when I became aware that I was being used and not respected and when I realized how short life is and that my happiness was more important than assuaging my guilt for having married for the wrong reasons.

I wanted to live with passion and purpose. I wanted to live

without fearing and dreading another false, cold tomorrow. The stress and conflict I experienced in my marriage was in direct opposition to my living this way. But the crumbling marriage, the dying father, illuminated truths I couldn't see otherwise. These truths, shifting my perspective, helped me discover self-confidence and recognize my burning desire to change my situation.

These three are the necessities for approaching life differently, for making deliberate and lasting changes, and for living a life of purpose and passion without fear. They interact and reinforce each other, as this portrait of them shows, when we summon them to free us from our comfort zones, and from the traps we fall into when we don't question the plan.

Let's explore where these catalysts already are in your life, and how you can discover and claim them.

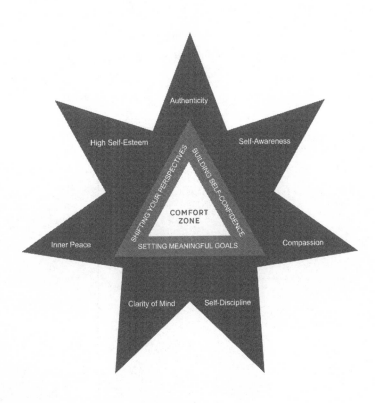

Authenticity

High Self-Esteem

Self-Awareness

SHIFTING YOUR PERSPECTIVES

BUILDING SELF-CONFIDENCE

COMFORT ZONE

Inner Peace

SETTING MEANINGFUL GOALS

Compassion

Clarity of Mind

Self-Discipline

YOUR THREE CATALYSTS

CENTERING

- Seat yourself comfortably.

- Open your hands, facing your palms upward.

- Close your eyes.

- Inhale through your nose for a count of 3; exhale through your nose for 6.

- As you repeat this breathing pattern, notice areas of tightness in your body.

- Let the tension melt away.

- Prepare yourself to receive the gifts of this moment, of your situation, of your existence.

- Smile as you breathe in these gifts.

- Exhale with appreciation for what you receive. You need not see or know what these gifts are, simply be open and receive.

- Continue smiling as you breathe in your gifts and as you exhale with appreciation.

- Acknowledge your joy.

- Continue breathing, receiving, and appreciating as long as you'd like.

- When you feel ready, take one last deep breath, and say to yourself "abundance."

- Open your eyes slowly as you exhale.

- You are now ready.

EXPLORING

1. Think about a change you'd like to make in your life.

    Write down exactly what you would like to change. This could be the change you wrote about in the first activity or it could be something completely different.

    Why is making this change important to you? Consider these questions and write what comes to you about them:

    *   How will you benefit?

    *   What will you gain?

2. Change is rooted in our own individual values. Here are some that may come into play in your own explorations. Choose three to five that seem important to this change you want to make.

VALUE	VALUE	VALUE
Accomplishment	Friendship	Privacy
Abundance	Fulfillment	Professionalism
Achievement	Fun	Recognition
Adventure	Holistic Living	Respect
Altruism	Honesty	Romance
Autonomy	Humor	Security
Beauty	Integrity	Self-Care
Clarity	Intimacy	Self-Expression
Commitment	Joy	Self-Mastery
Communication	Leadership	Self-Realization
Community	Loyalty	Sensuality
Connecting to others	Nature	Service
Creativity	Openness	Simplicity of Life
Emotional Health	Orderliness	Spirituality
Environment	Peace	Trust
Excellence	Personal Growth	Truth
Family	Partnership	Vitality
Flexibility	Physical Appearance	Walking the Talk
Freedom	Power	Other

- Review your chosen values and consider your first step in making this change.

» Write out what this first step is.

» Of your chosen values, what is the one that most strongly urges you to take this first step? Circle that value.

- Write out why this value moves you into action. Be as specific as you can about what it means to you and why you chose it as the strongest.

- Consider these questions and write about them:
    » How does this value move you to act?

    » Is the action you considered as a first step based on this value?

    » Does your action arise from the desire to achieve the goal and benefits you explored above, or does it simply help you avoid a negative consequence?

- Write about this value's importance to you, and to your action:
    » How does this value tell you to act?

    » How might acting on this value help you take the first step? How might it hinder you from taking a first step?

    » How might using this value as a motivator help you see this change through to completion? How might it hinder you from completing this change?

3. Now consider the change you wanted to make. Imagine you have outlined all the steps to make this change. Write down the answers these questions bring:

- Think about taking the very first step to implement this change—what thoughts and feelings come to mind?
- How will your environment, your skills, constraints of time and money, ties to friends and family, and their reactions to this change foster or hinder taking this step.
- How will these foster or hinder seeing the change through to completion?
- Visualize yourself actually taking that first step. Write down your thoughts and emotions as you do so.

4. Considering those thoughts and emotions, write out your answers to the following questions.
   - Were your thoughts positive, empowering, and inspiring? Did they make you want to do more than just think about taking that first step?
   - Were they negative and stifling, full of apathy or dread? Did they discourage you from considering that first step?
   - Or were they some combination of optimism and pessimism? Which was stronger?
   - What do those thoughts and emotions say about you and your readiness to make this change?

5. To ponder how those thoughts and emotions might color your approach to making this change, write down answers to these questions:
   - If your thoughts were mostly positive,
     » How can you use them to start this change?
     » How can you bring them to bear if, after you've

gotten started, you encounter setbacks, doubts, or
discouragement?

- If your thoughts were mostly negative, what limitations did
  they bring up? These limitations are real for you right now;
  they offer information about your perspective and about what
  action you can take. It is important to examine them:
    » What specific worries or fears did you experience?
    » What were you concerned might or might not happen?
    » What were you afraid you might lose?

- If your thoughts were limiting, take three deep cleansing
  breaths.
    » Imagine that you have just awakened from an invigorating
      night's rest. As you open your eyes, refreshed, you sense
      that something has changed. You realize that those limita-
      tions and blocks to reaching your goal have miraculously
      vanished, and you have successfully reached your goal.
    » Write down how that feels to you.
    » Write down how you feel after writing about that.

MAPPING

1. Think about the change you listed in the Exploring section of this
   activity. Write out what successfully completing it looks like to you.
   Consider the following:
   - What must be part of this successful change for you to feel
     satisfied with your accomplishment?

- How will you know if you've succeeded? Describe what success must include.

2. Picture yourself taking the first step to make this change.
    - Write out what's going through your mind when you envision reaching the success you just envisioned. Consider the following questions:
        » Do you feel confident in your ability to complete the change successfully?
        » Can you picture yourself reaping the rewards of making this change?
        » Do you feel excited about getting started?
        » Or are you thinking of ways to delay getting started?
        » Are you feeling dread about taking that first step?
        » Are you telling yourself that it's too hard, or that you failed before, so why bother?
    - Read through what you've written. Write down what is most important about it to you.

3. If you're feeling confident and positive, run with these thoughts.
    - Use them to map out your plan for this change and begin.

4. If you're telling yourself you can't accomplish this, think of another challenge that faced you, something you didn't think you could accomplish but you did.
    - List the things you did to make yourself a success. (Maybe you practiced, planned, or got encouragement or advice from

someone with more experience in the undertaking.) Consider how you reached success in the past.

- Review these strategies for success, and circle the two or three that seem most useful in helping you make the change you want to make.

- What does it look like when you use these ideas to improve your chances? Write down the improvements they help you make. Write down how your chances for success look after that.

- Having completed this set of activities, take another couple of minutes and write down your feelings.

Congratulations on your explorations! It is now time to claim what you've discovered. Claim it even if you don't believe it. It is yours: your very personal insight into yourself and into your perspective, confidence, and desire.

CLAIMING

- Seat yourself in a comfortable position and close your eyes.

- Breathe in through your nose and out through your nose as you have done in the previous centering exercises.

- As you let go of any lingering troubling thoughts or emotions, let the muscles in your face, neck, and shoulders go limp.

- Continue breathing as you focus on the wave of relaxation that is flowing down through your arms, your hands, your fingers, your chest, your belly, your legs, your feet, your toes.

- Notice any sensations you feel—warmth or cold, ease or constraint, expansion or tightness.

- Breathe confidence into yourself. Breathe doubt out.
- Breathe in courage. Breathe out fear.
- Breathe in boldness. Breathe out constriction.
- Continue to breathe in all that is positive and release what traps, limits, or no longer serves you.
- When you feel ready, take one last deep breath in, and say to yourself, "I am confidence. I am courage. It is mine."
- Open your eyes slowly as you exhale.
- Congratulate yourself on a job well done.

Exploring and mapping can feel difficult, or even frightening, because they cross the borders of what you might currently believe is possible. Simply experiencing a shift, real or imagined, however, starts to change how your mind works, and, more importantly, shifts your perspective.

The more often you create such shifts, the more familiar your mind becomes with this process, the easier it will be for you to see things, especially yourself and your situation, differently. Those changes in perspective make it more likely that the constraints you feel in self-image, and about what is possible for you in this world, will yield and free you.

The exploration gave you insight into what's important to you and brought awareness of what fears might be keeping you stuck, safe, and small. Values, our guiding principles, motivate us to do what we do, and live as we live. As I've learned, not only in my own life, but from those whom I've coached, we hold two types of values—those based in bold self-awareness that move us to experience something, and those based in fearful self-limitation that move us to avoid something. If we can identify our fear-based values, we can become aware of them, evaluate their importance, and release their hold on us.

Mapping helps you uncover limiting beliefs about your abilities, repercussions you may fear when making a change, and other perceptions you hold about the world and your environment that block your success in making changes in your life. When you shine a light on these limitations, you begin to take away their power. Recognizing them not only brings you awareness, it allows you to examine, understand, and move past them.

These activities are part of your quest for boldness. They are a continuing source of insight and power, and can be part of the process whenever you start on a goal, or make a change, and certainly whenever you feel stuck. Writing out and rereading your thoughts and feelings using these activities frees your mind, reminds you what is most important to you, and lights the way to your next steps and better decisions.

CHAPTER 3
LIFT THE VEIL

*The range of what we think and do is limited by what we fail to notice.
And because we fail to notice that we fail to notice, there is little we can do to
change; until we notice how failing to notice shapes our thoughts and deeds.*
—R. D. Laing

Everything we know, and everything we think we know, gives us our view of ourselves and the world. Everything we know, and everything we think we know, blinds us to ourselves and the world. Our experiences and beliefs arise, as Laing points out, from what we notice—and what we don't. Our unique perspective isn't bad or wrong, it's simply incomplete, because we can't know or see the whole story. That limitation limits our grasp of what's possible in the world, and in ourselves. Until circumstances force us, or lead us toward, what we haven't noticed, we will live within those boundaries. Where we can get stuck.

The ability to shift perspective plays a huge role in this process of growing bold, and in living the life you choose. So many I meet call me bold because of the things I'm doing. As it turns out, they, too, have considered following their own dreams and living life on their own terms. They've repeatedly eliminated those possibilities. Overlooking their blind spots, they've listened to their limits, silently and effectively preventing their own efforts.

Their blind spots—what they couldn't see—supplied them with reasons not to question the plan and live their own lives. My approach to life attracts them; they feel that their lives, too, would be better if they could adopt this approach. When they call me bold, it is a compliment, a generous, often admiring, acknowledgment of the choices I've made. But in another way, this acknowledgment is sad, because it is an admission they can't see those possibilities in themselves.

The universe, including people, moves. Energy powers us, as it does stars, planets, plants, and animals. Our senses focus on the energies around us, bringing us news about how things look, smell, taste, and feel. We can't see this energy, but we can feel it—as sound, it causes the air to move, or vibrate.

Energy of all kinds vibrates at higher or lower rates, or frequencies. The thoughts that cause neurons in our brains to fire are themselves a form of psychic energy, an energy powerful enough to move us—or to trap us.

Coarse, harsh thoughts proceed slowly, like deeper, lower-frequency sounds: *Why can't I ever get a break? I've got to fight for what is mine.* These thoughts recur like a refrain, a changeless set of assumptions that can keep us heavy, sluggish, or depressed, that can drain, or even destroy, our power to move.

Lighter, easier thoughts move more quickly: *How can we make this situation work for us? Let's not focus on what we can't do, let's focus on what we can do.* They change as we entertain them, opening us to constructive, creative possibilities. They restore us and help us move ahead.

If we can change perspectives, shifting from our less productive, heavier thoughts and self-assessments to others that include our higher goals and untried possibilities, we harness an energy that moves not only our worldview but our lives. We notice what went unnoticed before, and tap resources unseen before in ourselves, and in the world.

CLEAR THE SCREEN

Our perspective is the screen between us and everything outside us. Our emotions and convictions, our religion, our values, our heritage, our education, the facts we know, the skills we have, our culture, our family life, our ideas, and the way all these elements interrelate in our minds, shape this perspective. Through it we view the world and our own lives, and, more importantly, our goals and expectations, as well as our limits, those we impose on ourselves, and those imposed by our situation.

Consider, for example, the perspectives, of Harry, Ann, and Ophelia, who just now received layoff notices from Major Industries, Inc. Harry, 25, a recent college graduate, feels dejected. This has happened twice before, and now he believes he is jinxed. Ann, 55, is angry. Several friends her age have also lost their jobs. She read about age discrimination in the workplace and concluded that this caused her layoff. Ophelia, 35, has been considering a career change. This news frees her to pursue the idea instead of just thinking about it.

Each individual's personality, education, and experiences chains or frees energy, moves or hampers progress. Even knowing as little as you do right now about Harry, Ann, and Ophelia, you can already see that each one's search for a new job will follow a different path and yield different results.

Our assessments of our situation are enmeshed in our perspectives. The more judgmental we are (*I'm jinxed, or They think I'm old*), the narrower our perspective will be, and the more negative our outlook. Negative thoughts take our energies lower and lead us into low-energy circumstances. If we believe, like Harry, that things happen because we're jinxed, or no good, we may also believe that our efforts are futile. Harry thinks life is a rigged game; he can't win, so why play?

This low-energy perspective suggests no actions and limits his choices: *Why does this always happen to me? Why am I the one they always pick? Last time it took me a whole year to find a job that I was overqualified for.* Despondent, Harry retreats. He applies for a few jobs, but soon gives up.

Ann's perspective is different, but equally narrow: *They decided to dump me because I'm more experienced and earn more than younger, less-experienced workers. Even my 40-year-old boss doesn't have my qualifications. It's unfair. I'll show them! They can't treat me like this. I'll sue, get what's mine, and give them bad publicity.* If we believe that someone has harmed or threatened us, we may feel violated or even attacked.

Feelings of blame, anger, and self-righteousness arise, forcing us to fight back and defend ourselves. We obsess about getting even. Ann's lawsuit, and even more, Ann's thirst for revenge, will consume her time and energy so thoroughly that she won't be able to seek a new opportunity.

If, in moments of setback or crisis, we can set aside our negative thoughts and feelings about a situation and take a less rigid position about events, we make room for a shift in perspective. Multiple explanations for what has occurred come to us, along with many more solutions. Our attitude changes, we feel more hopeful and positive, and our energy rises, too: life seems to flow more easily.

After she takes some time to assimilate the unexpected news, Ophelia thinks, *This layoff was unfortunate, but the company had to do it to save many other jobs. I was ready for a change anyway. Because they terminated me rather than asking me to resign, I can train myself in a new field with my severance money, and I can pay some of my living expenses with unemployment.* Ophelia has already begun working toward her new career. She will quickly meet people who can help her along.

How harshly we judge ourselves and others, along with how

much stress we feel, shadows or brightens our worldview and our grasp of available options. Harry's worldview might be even worse if he's under financial stress and doesn't have emergency savings. Ann might be even angrier if her husband of thirty years just left her. And Ophelia might be less hopeful if she's developed a serious illness and needs a job with good health insurance.

Outside circumstances, especially stress, also affect our responses to new situations, especially if these appear to be setbacks. Working to lower stress and anxiety through exercise, proper nutrition, and meditation not only helps us see the bigger, more positive picture, it helps changes in perception to happen more readily and allows us to act upon them more easily.

As Harry, Ann, and Ophelia illustrate, our perspectives can limit or improve our lives. Shifts to the positive increase possibilities, making us feel happier, freer, and aware of more choices, while shifts to the negative limit and blind us to what might be possible.

To live a bold life, try consciously to shift every perspective to the positive, moving out of depressing low-energy depths to restorative, high-energy, creative heights. Making this shift on purpose is the first step toward boldness. Doing so successfully makes us feel good, start moving, and see various paths forward.

As you've seen already, and as your own explorations in Chapters 1 and 2 have shown you, all kinds of occurrences, inner and outer, can fuel these shifts: accidents; disasters; deaths; awe-inspiring or moving events; reflection; new information. And layoffs, of course, as Harry, Ann, and Ophelia know. I know about them, too.

In my first job out of college, I got fired. This shifted my perspective radically, and negatively, taking me from annoyance to full-blown outrage, apparently overnight. The company had hired two of us as management trainees. Although we went through the same training program and started work the same day, he got his own desk, chair, and telephone.

My situation was different. I shared table space with the microfiche reader, a hulking machine the size of a TV set. It left so little space that I did any writing necessary on a pad on my lap. Coworkers needed the machine constantly. Rather than interrupting or displacing me, they waited until I went to lunch. When I returned, they scattered, underlining my sense of being an inconvenient, menial intruder. I asked myself if this was what I went to college for.

My parents, who came of age during the Civil Rights struggle, remained alert to overt and covert racism. I did not share their concern until, after many attempts to secure fair treatment at work, I lost my job. In that moment, I thought, *Mommy and Daddy were right. My skin color is a cross I must bear, and a cause I must fight for, if I want the things taken from me restored.* Racism, I realized, was not eradicated. My indignation at not being given space to do the work for which I'd been hired exploded into rage, and I fought back.

I built a case against my former employer and filed it with the Equal Employment Opportunity Commission. Documentation, deadlines, affidavits, arguments, insults, and a pervasive feeling of grievance replaced frustration, helplessness, and isolation. Eight long, acrimonious months later, I won. My former employer agreed to a financial settlement.

Despite the money, however, I didn't feel victorious. Or vindicated. Instead, I still felt defeated and dissatisfied. My case, and more than that, my desire to get back at my employer, had consumed me, stealing my energy and trapping me in revenge, which stopped me in my tracks and kept me looking backward, the narrowest trap of all.

It took me nine months to pull myself together and find another job, a job for which I turned out to be overqualified. In the end, I realized, winning not only didn't make me happier, it made me less able to look at events as offering choices.

The job stress, and the layoff, caused a shift in my perspective, but that shift took me further down—from the depression and apathy of a difficult workplace to an almost limitless anger that ate me up inside. This perspective moved me to act—or, rather, to react, keeping me trapped in the past, trying to rewrite events that had already happened. The suit was "successful," but this success didn't satisfy me or help me feel that I was in charge of my own life. Thoughts of revenge brought with them a self-righteous attitude that blinded me to the range of other choices I really had.

I could have looked for another job right away, instead of

fighting the company; I could have taken a different approach to getting the fair treatment I wanted; I could even have let management know I was prepared to sue, and why, using my situation to help them see what fairness really meant. Years later, when I saw that there really were other choices, and that I had unwittingly trapped myself by seeing only the most negative, I understood the whole episode more clearly.

Even now, decades later, thinking about that time and about what my life was like then brings me low. I unconsciously shifted my perspective to what I decided I'd lost, and how to get payback, rather than giving myself the time, and the permission, to ponder these events.

What *might* have happened if I'd shifted to the positive, to thoughts of release and of other possible options? *This was for the better, I hated that job. Plenty of companies out there will hire me and respect me for who I am and what I offer. Good thing I'm living at home, at least I don't have to worry about paying the rent.*

I admit it would have been a stretch for me to be this positive and trusting then, but now, after years of experience, I *know* that if I could have shifted to different, more positive thoughts, things would have played out differently, and likely better. Years later, I had an experience that showed me the value of moving to higher, more positive energy.

After working at a financial services company for several years as a full-time permanent employee, I left to pursue another opportunity. I returned, however, and landed a project manager spot. The drawback was that this was a two-year contract position rather than a permanent one, which disappointed me at first.

As I settled into the job, though, I came to be happy that our relationship would end in just two years. The company had grown tremendously; it was a very different organization from the one I'd left earlier to be my own boss. As I consider this situation now, I see the irony of landing at the place I'd left when I was trying to escape my choice of career, as if this second encounter were expressly designed to test my ability to make a life-changing shift in perspective.

When the company recruited me and interviewed me for this position, the hiring manager seemed delighted with my experience and credentials. During the years I'd worked elsewhere, I'd earned an MBA, Project Management Professional certification, plus a master's certificate in project management. She found these very desirable and hired me at a very nice hourly rate.

Her eagerness to hire an experienced project manager suggested I'd be involved in the company's more complex projects, helping to plan, develop, or direct them. As I soon learned, however, full-time project managers got those high-pro-file roles, building a set of substantial accomplishments to cite on their performance self-appraisals. They were on the way up, and these projects were their ladder.

The company had no interest in building my résumé—I was just a temporary employee, and mine was a dead-end job. So I found myself serving as support staff on these projects—scheduling meetings and taking notes during them: an assistant; a bridesmaid, not a bride.

I wanted projects I could sink my teeth into, and I wanted more responsibility. But it was time to move forward and make the best of the situation, I recognized that. As I'd been unable to do in that first job, I reframed my perspective on the situation, appraised myself and my choices, and prepared to let go.

I chose to throw myself into the work and to become a valuable resource on the projects I supported. I observed how the project leaders approached risks and solved problems, and I learned. By diligently providing the necessary help, I became someone my project teams looked forward to seeing every day. By taking the high road, I made the work more pleasant and tolerable not only for myself, but for my coworkers. Shifting perspective helped me see past my own limitations, allowing me to raise my eyes from others' goals and requirements to my own.

Now we'll explore perspective shifts in more depth, for they are an essential catalyst. Your explorations in the next few pages, and throughout this book, will help you experience such shifts emotionally and imaginatively, preparing you to change your worldview and your life. Take as long as you need. If you need more time and space, take a break, re-center yourself, and return.

ADJUST YOUR SIGHT

CENTERING

- Seat yourself comfortably.
- Close your eyes.
- Breathe in deeply through your nose for a count of 3; exhale through your nose for 6.
- As you breathe, allow your entire body to relax.
- Say to yourself, "There is no right or wrong. It just is."
- Breathe in vitality, breathe out constriction.
- Breathe and allow the spirit inside you to be free.
- Enjoy the energy you receive in this moment for as long as you like.
- When you feel ready, take one last deep breath.
- As you exhale, say to yourself "I am the author of my story. I am the master of my destiny."
- Open your eyes.
- You are ready.

EXPLORING

1. Think back to a time when you were subjected to a change that was forced upon you.
   - What was the situation? Describe it in writing.

2. Write out how you reacted to that change.
   - What were your thoughts?
   - How did you feel?
   - What did you do?

3. In thinking back on this event, what do you notice about how it shifted your energy and perception of the world? What option(s) seemed available to you?

MAPPING

1. If your energy and perceptions were on the negative, draining side (thoughts of despair and hopelessness or anger and conflict), consider now:
    * What thoughts could you have had that might have shifted your perspective and energy in the opposite direction?
    * Was there struggle or flow in the aftermath of this change?

2. If your thoughts were on the positive, energizing side (thoughts of hopefulness, opportunity, enthusiasm or excitement), consider now:
    * What allowed you to stay above negative thoughts and not be pulled in by them?
    * What were the results of your positive response?
    * Was there struggle or flow in the aftermath of this change?

3. Write out what you learned about yourself from this activity.

CLAIMING

* Breathe in deeply through your nose for a count of 3; exhale through your nose for 6.
* Close your eyes.
* As you continue to breathe consciously, give thanks for your life, your decisions, the challenges and opportunities.

- Give thanks for the journey that has led you to where you are today.
- Smile to yourself.
- When you are ready, take one last deep breath in.
- As you exhale, congratulate yourself on a job well done. There is no right or wrong. Our experiences just are.

SHED THE PAST

We are born with self-confidence, the belief that we have it in ourselves to achieve what we set our minds to. Experience sometimes erodes or even seems to destroy this essential attitude. We come to fear making mistakes, or to dread others' opinions. These fears, and our own negative experiences, trample our courage and teach us to doubt our abilities. We can, however, renew that early self-confidence. We have simply forgotten it, burying its radiance beneath doubt and self-judgment. Excavating that early faith in ourselves, remembering it, can help us restore it again.

Setting goals that mean something to us, and working toward them despite temporary failures, calls back our belief in ourselves. Part of this process is becoming aware of those negative and fearful thoughts, learned through pain, that we play and replay in our minds. Awareness disarms them, leaving room to replace them with thoughts that strengthen and encourage us.

These two steps, pursuing our goals and revising what we tell ourselves, not only help us achieve our goals, they restore our conviction that we *can* achieve. Reaching our goals, in turn, proves to ourselves, and to others, that we *can* achieve. Thoughts that contradict our fears not only lead us forward, they carry us through as we accomplish things we might have felt we couldn't.

As adults, we've learned far more than we realize about a tremendous variety of subjects in a wide range of fields. We have set and reached all sorts of goals. Even so, and despite all this very real learning and accomplishment, many adults I work with have surprisingly little faith in themselves.

As children we learned almost spontaneously to walk, talk, run, read, write—an endless array of accomplishments. We did so without hesitation, self-doubt, or fear. Imagine trying to learn all that today. Our adult minds, chock-full of discouraging thoughts and negative experiences, lavishly supplied with fear of risk, with humiliation and failure, might paralyze us so thoroughly we couldn't try. *What if I fall? I'll look inept and people will laugh at me. I'll be ridiculed and rejected. Or worse yet, what if I fall and break a bone or hit my head? I could hurt myself seriously and be worse off than I am now.*

Most children never contend with these what-ifs, or give themselves over to negative possibilities. They don't think like this. Babies and young children try fearlessly. They fail again and again until they succeed. They keep after their goals. They move along by moving, as a baby learns to walk by grasping furniture for support. That practice leads to skill, and soon the baby lets go and walks. Strengthened by success, the toddler moves on to the next experience.

RECLAIM THE POWER

After I reframed my perspective as a contractor, the company and my coworkers benefited from my improved outlook; so did I. Changing the way I saw the situation changed how I acted, letting me focus more clearly on the work at hand. Despite feeling uninspired by the work, I learned and grew. This boosted my self-confidence.

But how did I make that shift? I knew that my contract would expire, and I knew when. Those facts prepared me to leave my ill-fitting project manager job almost from the beginning. Before I could work out my next steps, though, a new perspective hit me like lightning.

Life has caused many shifts, sometimes after changes outside my control (*parents won't live forever, and neither will I, therefore I must stop playing at life*), sometimes after the gradual appearance of new viewpoints (*public speaking isn't really dreadful; it can actually be fun*). Usually, though, shifts take time and self-examination. This particular change in my thinking, sudden and memorable, came while reading a book.

I knew it was time to move forward. As I'd been unable to do in my first job out of college, I prepared to let go. To help gather myself, I browsed the work of Stuart Wilde, a New Age philosopher. This passage caught my eye:

If you want to be accepted, accept yourself. If you want to be acknowledged, acknowledge yourself. Simple.

I'd heard and read similar sentiments before, but these sentences struck me. The way he expressed these truths, and the place where I was in my life, made me unusually receptive. I longed so much for challenge and needed so deeply to grow that I added my own words to his: *If you want to be challenged, challenge yourself.*

The seed, once planted, sprouted overnight. I would create a challenge for myself, making it easier to endure the monotony and irritation at work. A challenge could be my life jacket, floating me through until my contract ended and I moved on to better things.

"If you want to be challenged, challenge yourself." When I said it, I felt strong, strength that sent me looking for a challenge to tackle. Two afternoons later, on my third cup of coffee, which I needed because I felt tired all the time, and fighting the scratchy cough and congestion of raging allergies, the challenge appeared: I would eat more healthfully, which might ease the allergies and help me shed a few pounds in the process.

I took a cold, clear look at the quite substantial woman I'd become. Deep-dish pizza, pasta, Chinese food, chips, cookies, and cakes did that, the filling, delicious, stress-reducing, waist-line-enlarging treats that fueled my team's late-night sessions in the project command center. Food helped us weather the hours of planning and organizing, and the tension and pressure of rushing against deadlines.

Team spirit, late hours, project requirements, and especially the food, the food, the food, presented tremendous obstacles. I wasn't sure if I could overcome them. I walked through other possibilities, but this challenge, like that passage in the book, kept ringing inside me, insisting on its importance. As I pondered how to answer it, I summoned earlier experiences, earlier successes.

Fifteen years before, week by week, ounce by ounce, I'd lost fifty pounds with Weight Watchers. Recalling that challenge, and also how good it felt to drop all that weight, helped me give the obstacles less power.

They were, after all, only aspects of something else I didn't have much control over, my job. Losing weight, however, was something I did have power over: the power to choose or not to choose my own health and well-being. I set my mind on succeeding, and I called back other successes.

Fall's crisp air, the leaves' bright warm colors, signal a time of change. This has always been my favorite season—except once. That particular fall, midway through my junior year of college, I sat in the car, closed away from the bracing air and brilliant leaves, sobbing with frustration and despair. I'd failed.

The macroeconomics comprehensive exam, the last obstacle between me and my economics degree, had beaten me. My college career was over. It was the end of the world. Nothing could help me now. I had to face the truth: I just wasn't smart enough for college after all. Slumped in the seat that gorgeous day, I presided as judge and jury of my life, my education, my hopes, and my dreams, and the verdict was death.

Gloom and doom might well have stopped me if Terri, a fellow econ major, hadn't happened by. She observed my meltdown but, unaware of its cause, gave me space. Later that day, she sent me an encouraging note. When I thanked her, I admitted that I'd flunked the comp. "Yeah," she said. "Econ is a tough major. But don't forget, you already made it through the required classes. I know you'll pass this exam next time."

"Next time." Her comment stopped me in my tracks. I'd been so focused on disaster and inadequacy, I hadn't even considered the possibility of retaking the test. This crash didn't have to be fatal. I could try again. It was a setback, certainly, but it didn't have to be the final verdict. Terri helped me find a more useful perspective, and she recalled, too, previous successes. I picked myself up, learned the material—failing the test had shown me what to study harder—did well the next time, and earned the degree.

Remembering that success, along with my earlier success with Weight Watchers, encouraged me to tackle the diet. But those achievements were long ago. I wondered if I still had that resilience and willpower, or whether the stress of unsatisfying work and tight deadlines would throw me off balance and derail my determination to control my own life.

Casting about for more recent evidence, I considered all that I'd accomplished in settling my father's affairs a few months before. That process certainly combined a challenge with stress and anxiety. My father's finances were disorderly; I untangled them and tied up the loose ends. I cleaned out his house, a three-story Victorian, including its jam-packed basement, driving the 250 miles each way as often as necessary. I got the house repaired and maintained it until it sold. All that time, I did an excellent job at work. All that time, too, I mourned his death.

Two weeks before Daddy died, he drew up his will. He turned to me and asked, "Would you do me the honor of being executrix of my estate?"

"Of course," I'd said. A naïve answer, as it turned out, another moment life stepped in to teach me. I wanted so much to do the last thing he asked, and I wanted to do it well. Soon, though, I realized that settling things was a huge undertaking. Reluctantly, but sure it was the right thing to do, I hired an estate attorney to piece the financial situation together and to challenge erroneous charges. I asked relatives and friends for help cleaning out the house.

Weekly surprises punctuated my efforts—his bank accounts were empty, the powder room sprang a leak, flooding the whole downstairs, a member of the cleaning crew gashed his head open on a cabinet, and unscrupulous movers dumped Daddy's furniture on my front lawn. Still, despite difficult work and tight deadlines, I resolved each problem. I tied every loose end. I sold the house.

All this was evidence. The determination and persistence that helped me succeed on the exam and lose the earlier weight also gave me the strength to help my father through his last illness, and to take care of his estate. This evidence, past and present, showed me I could take on my new challenge and succeed, and helped me remember that a temporary defeat was not a final failure, and reminded me to seek support when I needed it at Weight Watchers meetings.

On a sunny March day, I signed up with Weight Watchers. Things started inauspiciously: I gained almost a pound that first week. I stuck with it, though, and lost six pounds the first month. More important, I resisted the temptation of those free meals at work. Knowing that I had the power to choose encouraged me onward.

Resisting wasn't always easy, though. After months planning the steps, the day came for our project team to migrate two call centers to a new customer-servicing system. We'd sent on-site technical teams to the centers, while ten other team members, including me, staffed the War Room. The migration launched flawlessly.

When lunchtime came, I ate a garden salad from the cafeteria while everyone else enjoyed burritos and tacos. As we chowed down, congratulating ourselves on the smooth transition, one of the tech teams called in: the system was not working right. Key information didn't appear on the screen, meaning that our phone associates couldn't take care of our customers.

The War Room team went into high gear, mapping the situation out on whiteboards and trying to determine whether the problem was isolated or systemic. Tension gathered like a storm cloud, filling the room. I knew I'd be working far later than planned.

By four p.m., after frustration built and tempers flared and died, we'd decided to roll back to the old system until we could pinpoint the cause. By then, having ranked our difficulties in order of urgency and dealt with those we could solve, I'd burned off my salad. Hunger fought with anxiety; the project wasn't going as planned, a problem that also threatened my diet.

I hadn't anticipated working late, so I hadn't brought the healthful food I usually ate. I kicked myself mentally, realizing I'd have to dip into the Italian buffet already on its way—chafing dishes of meatball lasagna and eggplant parmesan, and multiple loaves of hot buttered garlic bread. My first WW test. How badly, I wondered, would I fail?

Ninety minutes later, when the food arrived, I was starving. The aroma shredded what little willpower remained. I caved with gusto, heaping my plate with lasagna and garlic bread and skipping the salad. After the day I'd had, I *deserved* a good meal. And dessert. After dinner, I felt satisfied, and calmer. A pang of guilt stabbed me, but I told myself, "I've got to eat, and this job is so stressful. This one slip is OK." The rest of the team was more subdued as well, gathering itself, as I was, to meet the work challenge.

Later, when we'd made some progress, and dinner had settled a bit, I helped myself to a cookie the size of my face. "You've blown the day," I murmured, "you might as well enjoy it. You can get back on track tomorrow." That was exactly what I did. The food hangover I felt the next day, sluggish after overeating, helped keep the goal before me.

That late-night session taught me to stock the right food for lunch and dinner. Of course, sometimes what I packed wasn't appealing compared to what the team ordered in. When that happened, I excused myself and ate elsewhere, away from temptation. After I was full, those high-calorie treats were easier to turn down. Or, occasionally, I indulged, but with restraint, eating half the normal amount and filling up with veggies. The more weight I lost, the more control I gained over my life; I had the power rather than food having it, and I also had the energy to continue my progress.

Thirteen months later, I was seventy-five pounds lighter. Boy, was I feeling strong! *If you want to be challenged, challenge yourself.* That surprise shift in perspective produced amazing results. A small movement away from depending on others to give me interesting work and from constant disappointment when they didn't, revolutionized everything.

I chose the challenge, and I met the challenge. Both were less important, really, than how free, and strong, succeeding made me feel. The boring, unsatisfying job stopped mattering, because I saw it from this vantage point of strength, full of confidence that I was in charge of my thoughts and emotions. Losing the weight, which grew from this sudden shift in perception, and the surprising, good changes that meeting the challenge brought were unimaginable. If I had not been open to thinking differently, they never would have happened.

Losing those extra pounds removed a wall, a shell that didn't protect but actually blocked my true self. That shell vanished. Not only do I have extra energy now, I feel better in every way—not just physically but mentally. In addition, shopping and dressing are fun now, because those cute outfits I find fit so well.

Choosing and meeting this challenge increased the awareness and self-control that already helped me grow bolder. Another reward was that success opened my mind to further possibilities, possibilities I now had the self-confidence to pursue.

Air travel was one. Flying as an overweight person was particularly unpleasant. After I squeezed painfully into those tight seats, my hips and legs still spilled over, touching the strangers who were my seatmates. This was so uncomfortable that I limited air travel to national conferences for my direct-sales job. Eventually, though, I stopped flying altogether.

After losing the weight, though, I considered flying again, this time for pleasure. I got a passport for the first time. I'd planned a summer trip to Amsterdam, but I had to cancel when my mother got sick. Instead, my first flight in ten years was to my twenty-fifth college reunion. I hadn't seen my classmates in years, and I was eager to get together. My walled-off, heavier self would have shot down that idea quickly and kept me home. Instead, I had a great time reconnecting with long-lost friends, some of whom I'm still in touch with.

The freedom to fly again was only one new possibility. Feeling like myself again also spurred me to find my voice again. As a teenager, I loved to write, but I'd put it down. After meeting the weight-loss goal, I signed up for a creative-writing class at a local college. That reminded me how much I'd enjoyed writing, how grounding and how cathartic it was. Writing—as your own experience in these pages has probably reminded you—is a tremendous way to shift perspective and to explore not only what is, but also what could be.

One class led to another, and another. I shared deeply personal stories with my classmates, hesitantly at first, but soon without apology or fear of judgment. The process of composing, revising, and reading was freeing. My true self revealed itself more and more fully on the page. My classmates' stories revealed that they, too, were experiencing this freedom. Their work, and mine, brought me into a world where I felt unique, yet intimately connected, a connection I'd longed for, especially after losing my mother. Those writing classes encouraged me into blogging as well as inspiring this book.

Freeing myself of the weight also freed me to let go. My mother's death left me alone in the house where she'd lived for three decades. Mom wasn't at all a hoarder, but over the years, things collected in closets, in the attic, in the garage. These were my things now. They had to go elsewhere, because the house was for sale.

I'd already cleared my father's house, choosing those things of his that connected me most closely to him. My modest house was full of his furniture, his curios, the pictures that hung on his walls. Now, a few years but many changes later, I did not feel compelled to hold on to most of my mother's things, even the remnants of my childhood. A few keepsakes were enough.

If it weren't for my new identity, or perhaps my old one resurfacing after the weight loss, I probably would have fretted over every object in her house, and clung to far too many of them. Returning to myself physically had clarified who I was and what I needed. I realized that my mother's things were not my mother, and weren't me, either. I arranged to give away, sell, or discard her belongings without anxiety or misgiving.

The confidence that meeting my weight-loss goal fostered also helped me purge many of my father's things, too. Some of them had turned my spare room into a large storage closet. Their departure meant I could transform that space into a bright, tranquil writing studio, my haven of creativity and peace.

———

The last chapter explored the idea that everything, including our thoughts about the world and ourselves, is energy. So often, our lives conform to our own estimate of our capacities, estimates that may be inaccurate or distorted. To live a bold life, we must reexamine not only what we believe about the world, but also what we believe about our abilities. Typically, those beliefs are negative and limiting. They belong to the past.

Even if those self-judgments were true for the person you were at that time (which is unlikely), you're different now. They're almost certainly not true for you today. Exposing and examining these long-held beliefs honestly is the first step toward expanding your abilities and mastering your situation.

To take a small example, someone who is chronically late despite repeated unsuccessful efforts to be punctual may conclude that he or she lacks organization, or willpower. That conclusion essentially predicts that punctuality will be impossible, no matter what.

That same person, may examine the internal message, however, and realize that these negative conclusions about organization and willpower aren't necessarily correct. Such examination leaves room to replace them with a less critical, less limiting, more positive message—*I do have control over what I do. Remember that spelling bee I studied for while all my friends played outside? I made a complicated study schedule for that, and met it. And I had the willpower to resist playing and reach the finals. I certainly* do *have willpower.*

Our level of faith in our abilities can influence who and what we attract into our lives, what goals we set, and how satisfied we are with life. Reframing obstacles or challenges as invitations rather than verdicts, as opportunities instead of barriers, is the first step toward overcoming rather than avoiding them.

These apparent obstacles can move us toward revising our view of ourselves and the world. When we reflect on our history, remembering times when we drew on our willpower, our intelligence, our knowledge, our skill to succeed, we change our outlook positively. We get unstuck, releasing our trapped energies—and we *move*. Doubt and frustration yield to inspiration and motivation.

Like questioning the plan, this move from judgment and pessimism to openness and optimism reveals unseen opportunities. These broader choices can increase our confidence, which in turn leads us to act on them. Changing our internal messages and setting ourselves up for success, however, go hand in hand. Our perceptions of the outer world and of ourselves must rise together. Blinding ourselves to possibilities means we can't take advantage of them. Lacking confidence to act means we can't make potential achievements real.

Some people see the world as offering grand opportunities—for others, but not for them, because they feel unworthy or incapable. They may indeed believe that daring or challenging action is possible, just not for them. A good friend, let's call her Lucia, has great faith in me and is genuinely excited about the way I live the life I've mapped out for myself. She says she *knows* I will make it happen. Her belief, in fact, inspires me to do more, to work harder.

"Why do you have so much faith in me?" I asked.

Lucia's answer? "You're different from me. You have something extra, something I don't." She truly believes that some extra ingredient or attribute, something she sees almost as a super-power, helps me turn dreams to reality.

"How can you have so much faith in me and so little in yourself?" I asked.

"You're different," she repeated. "I could never do what you're doing. I wouldn't know how to start." The truth is that she's the one with something extra: fear of failure. That fear steals her self-confidence and paralyzes her, keeping her where she is and as she is. To help her shed this, I've encouraged her to forgive herself and judge herself less harshly. I've also proposed that she try a very practical, immediate way to shed those past limitations by being willing to do something new badly. That's right: badly.

To grow bold, and to live a bold life, we must get used to trying new things, which means making mistakes and even, sometimes, failing. Trying new things offers new perspectives, but because they're new, we're likely to do them poorly at first.

If such an attempt fails, it was still successful in expanding your horizons. You played eighteen holes, even though each hole took ten strokes. Therefore, forgive yourself. It's okay. And if the attempt shows you that this new undertaking is something you want to be good at, you can always try again until you are good at it. That trying is practice.

If we can't forgive failure, we do more than inflict needless pain on ourselves, we stop trying, having judged ourselves incapable, or even unworthy, as Lucia does. Instead of growing bold, embracing and loving life, we simply grow old, cold, small, and grumpy.

My own fears centered on speaking up and seeming unintelligent. I used to struggle to converse. If I ever did answer someone's remarks, a wittier answer came to me seconds later. For the next few hours, I raked myself over the coals about what I should have said. As you can imagine, I was a quiet child, and a quiet young adult. Fear of saying the wrong thing silenced me.

I'm still shy. I still take time to think before I speak. But I don't fear misspeaking and I don't torment myself any more. I've stopped trying to impress others, or to win them over. I stopped imagining them as my judges, and stopped being my own judge, the harshest judge of all.

Instead, I've taught myself, through practice, to be kind to myself, to forgive myself: I am not in the movies; I don't have a script to follow; and I am not perfect. Words, after all, are breaths in the air. Now, if I say or do something clumsy or not quite clever, I let it go quickly, or amend it, let myself off the hook, and move along.

After I examined and reframed this fear of speaking, I set myself a challenge related to it, a small accomplishment to help me learn to speak up more easily. I'd planned a trip to Québec City, Canada, and I decided to learn French.

Though I'd taken high-school and college French, I never really worked at it, because I knew I would never be able to speak, read, or write French proficiently. I decided (based on no evidence) that my brother, who was fluent in German as well as French, and majored in comparative literature in college, got all the linguistic genes. I did just enough to pass, which was all I thought I was capable of.

The trip gave me a purpose for learning and a reason to challenge myself. I wanted to communicate with the locals in their beautiful language, and I welcomed the challenge. I set out to learn French using the Pimsleur Method, listening to and answering questions about the lessons for thirty minutes a day on my morning walk.

Despite the high probability that my answers would be wrong, and the even higher probability that I would look like a fool to passersby, I answered with authority. I didn't care about my mistakes or others' judgments. I wanted to learn, and this was how I was going to do it.

I gave myself permission to flub answers and mispronounce words. If negative thoughts crowded in when I messed up, I forgave myself the mistake and shooed away those thoughts by reminding myself that not only are mistakes normal when you try something new, they are part of the process of learning that new thing. Mistakes show us where we can improve.

After six weeks of lessons, I left for Canada. Though I was far from fluent and wished I'd started learning earlier, I was sure I could at least show respect to the Québécois and their country by speaking the French words and phrases I had mastered. Excited, I greeted those I met with hearty *bonjours*.

They wished me "Bonjour" in return, adding rapid-fire comments in French. When they caught me staring, clueless, they said, "Oh, you speak English. Your accent was so good it fooled me," which was thrilling!

Being unafraid to do something badly—in this case, to make mistakes learning French—freed me to work hard instead of doing the minimum. Learning without judging myself increased my confidence that I could learn. The compliments and encouragement of the native speakers boosted my confidence further, and also my desire to learn and improve. These successes encouraged me onward, and I've reached the intermediate level. I still practice daily, and still make mistakes, but the practice feels easier, and the mistakes are better mistakes, no longer those of a beginner.

UNLEASH YOUR POTENTIAL

CENTERING

- Seat yourself comfortably.
- Close your eyes.
- Breathe in deeply through your nose for a count of 3; exhale through your nose for a count of 6.
- As you inhale, breathe in positive energy, saying to yourself, "I am a positive light force."
- As you exhale, expel excuses, saying, "I release the lower energy within that blocks me."
- Breathe in love; breathe out fear. Breathe and embody the positive energy that you are.
- When you are ready, inhale deeply one more time, saying to yourself, "I am creative."
- Exhale, saying, "I allow my creativity to surround me."
- You are ready.

EXPLORING

1. What are you settling for because you feel life's doled it out to you and you haven't challenged it?
   - Describe one thing in your life that you are tolerating.

2. Tolerating implies that you would like this to be different. Why have you put up with this situation for as long as you have?
   - List all the reasons.

3. Review your reasons, which are your thoughts on the situation. Reframe your reasons 180°—to their opposites.

   Let's say you listed "I don't have time to work on building a second career."
   - Figure out and write down how much time you do have.
   - In that amount of time, what could you do to pursue a second career?

4. Review your reframed thoughts.
   - How do these new thoughts make you feel?
   - Write those feelings down.
   - What do these new thoughts bring up in you?
   - How might they help you take some action, no matter how small, to bring relief to what you are tolerating?

MAPPING

1. Think about one specific achievement that you are reluctant to try because you think you can't succeed.
   - What is that achievement? Describe it in detail, as specifically as you can.
   - Write out in a sentence or two what success would look like.

2. Now think about what holds you back, which fears, what negative or judgmental voice in your head says you can't or you shouldn't?
   - What exactly does it say to discourage you?
   - Write all the reasons you give yourself about why you can't accomplish this goal.

3. Consider this list. Look at the group of negative thoughts below, and choose those that most resemble the reasons on your list:

    a.   I've tried before and failed, so this time will be like those times.

    b.   Only people who have a certain quality or circumstance that I do not have (*fill in the blank—money; fame; education; a particular race, gender, or level of attractiveness*) can do that.

    c.   I'm not good enough to succeed at that.

    d.   The odds are against me.

    e.   I'm too (*fill in the blank—old, young, overweight, inarticulate, shy*) to achieve that.

4. Answer each negative thought you chose in writing.

- For a., *I've tried before and failed*, ask yourself:
  - » Why does this time have to be like the past?
  - » How am I different this time?

- For b., *Only people with a certain quality. . . .*, ask yourself:
  - » Where did that belief come from?
  - » How true is that belief?
  - » What other qualities do I have that could help me succeed?

- For c., *The odds are against me*, respond to these questions:
  - » What odds do I mean? To what statistics am I referring?
  - » What do I have going for me to increase my chances of success?
  - » How does *not* pursuing my goal benefit me?

» Does that benefit result from honoring a value based in fear or in conscious understanding? (See Chapter 2.)

» How does accomplishing my goal benefit me?

» Does that benefit result from honoring a value based in fear or in conscious understanding?

» Does the value honored by not pursuing this achievement conflict with the value honored by pursuing it?

» Look at the two values. Which is more important to you?

- For d., *I'm not good enough to be successful*, ask and respond to these:
  » When I say that I'm not good enough, in what specific ways am I not good enough—not smart enough, not outgoing enough, not talented enough, or not "whatever" enough? Write out your answer, giving examples.

- For e., I'm too . . . . , ask and respond to these:
  » "When I say that I'm too (fill in the blank), in what specific ways am I too _____?" Write out your answer, giving examples.

5. Reread your answer to question 2, about what holds you back, and to question 1, about an achievement you're reluctant to try.

- What are all the ways you could measure success in this undertaking?

- How would achieving even the smallest measure of success improve your sense of your ability and potential?

6. This exploration and mapping has helped you record your limiting beliefs on paper and question their validity. Now, shift gears:

   - As you think about this goal and the steps needed to work toward it, consider the very next task you can do toward reaching your goal.
   - Write it down, making sure this is a single task, not the completion of many tasks.

   (For example, if the goal means you need a college degree, the very next task wouldn't be to go to college; it might be to research schools, or to obtain an application, or to take an entrance exam.)

   Once you've defined this initial task, decide if you're ready to complete it. Otherwise, simply ponder it. This thoughtful consideration will help you know when you are ready, and help you take this step then.

7. Think of something you tried and wished you'd done better at.

   - Describe what you tried.

8. What, specifically, do you wish you had done better?

   - What would complete success have looked like?

9. Now consider the circumstances surrounding your attempt.

   - Why did you try this in the first place?
   - What previous experience did you have?
   - What did you believe about whether you could do this before

trying?

- What did you gain from trying?
- In what ways were you successful?

CLAIMING

- Seat yourself comfortably.
- Close your eyes.
- Inhale deeply through your nose for a count of 3; exhale slowly through your nose for a count of 6.
- Breathe deeply and relax.
- Breathe in courage; breathe out doubt.
- Feel that you are here to allow the perfection of the universe to unfold through your efforts.
- Breathe in deeply one more time.
- This time as you exhale, forgive yourself for not living up to your expectations.
- Write out, then say aloud:
  - "I did my best, given the circumstances, my beliefs, and my experience to that point."
  - "I have learned from it and take this lesson with me."
  - "This experience brought me personal growth. I release my negative thoughts about this trial, clearing my path to grow bold."
- Inhale deeply.
- Exhale, releasing all your negative thoughts.

Remembering our self-confidence is essential to living boldly. To regain and increase it, we must acquire the habit of shifting negative thoughts about ourselves to positive, strengthening ones. This shift includes forgiving ourselves for falling short of our own, often unrealistic, expectations. To learn and grow, we must try new things. When we try new things, we make mistakes. If we can forgive ourselves for these, they become our milestones toward improvement.

As Eckhart Tolle has said, "The great arises [from] small things . . . honored and cared for." This is true, too, of great confidence. Those who are accomplished, whether pianists, painters, or pitchers, amaze us with their skill. But their errors pointed to what they had to practice. The mastery we admire grew from hours, days, weeks, months, and years of mistakes and misfires.

The same trying, failing, and practicing that helped them become masters can help us, too, to build achievement, recover our self-confidence, and pursue our own bold journey.

CHAPTER 5
RUN WITH THE STARS

Marcus Aurelius, who spoke of time as a fast-moving river in the passage my mother read me, also suggested what our attitude should be as that river sweeps us along. "Dwell on the beauty of life. Watch the stars and see yourself running with them."

After I'd challenged myself and lost all that weight, the ingredients I needed for living with purpose had already gathered. Running with the stars, dwelling on the beauty of such a life was already possible. I just didn't look skyward. Soon, though, life opened my eyes.

ASSESS THE PATH

It was time to move on from that contract job. That necessity felt different this time. It didn't hurt, as it had when I lost that first job, or as I had hurt myself after fleeing into an unsuitable relationship so I could leave another job. When this contract reached its natural end, I took stock, instead of condemning myself or fretting about the future. What had changed, and why?

I had changed. I could measure the distance in some ways. I have always set and reached ambitious goals. At any point, I could probably explain quite coherently what these goals were and why they were important. But I hadn't really questioned the plan since leaving my marriage. I certainly hadn't considered my destination. I wanted to accomplish things—big things, but those goals I shot for didn't seem to fit together or suggest any particular endpoint or accomplishment. Something drove me, but something I couldn't explain. Something I couldn't always even see.

Somehow those goals were also mysterious. I worked toward them at the office, and even in my personal life, but now, as I sought perspective, I had to admit that even when I reached them, I didn't feel especially happy. This was disconcerting. And, as the contract job wound down, I also had to admit that, although I wasn't in pain, which was an improvement, I wasn't excited or pleased, either.

Thoughts of the future elicited a familiar doggedness mixed with sadness, rather than exhilaration or hope. I resisted wasting time or energy with these feelings, resolving to shift my perspective and see if I could discover why, despite so much that seemed different, and better, this crossroads still felt more like a dead end.

Eventually, I realized the truth; unemployment didn't cause

my unease. What I dreaded was the slog of time and trouble to find another job, and the drudgery of meeting that new job's goals—more goals that didn't feel like they belonged to me, more achievements in which I took no satisfaction.

I'd long worked a second job as a sales consultant with a direct-marketing business. I did not look at this work as career-building, so I could consider it more dispassionately. This business trained us to demonstrate its products, which we sold to interested clients. The consultation was free, the demonstration private. I asked myself if that job, too, raised these same negative feelings.

My first answer was: I felt good about this work. Direct sales fit me, because, for the most part, I worked for myself, and for the business. I liked setting my own schedule, my own goals, and my own strategies for meeting those goals. I was glad I didn't have to shepherd others toward outside deadlines and benchmarks as I did in my full-time job.

My next answer was: *not always good*. That answer, which arose when I took a truer measure of events, when I readjusted my perspective, forced me to think, to stand outside my present situation and ask myself what happened earlier in that job, and what was different now.

As with Weight Watchers, I'd enjoyed being recognized at meetings; I'd enjoyed doing sales demos, and attending sales trainings. I'd enjoyed showing clients the products, and I took great pleasure in the way these products improved clients' lives and their outlook. My regard for my clients, and my relationships with them, not any sales-pitch or pressure, spurred their purchases and made me successful.

That direct-sales job felt so rewarding that I considered pursuing advancement. The next step up, becoming a director, meant leading a unit of sales consultants. "I'm not sure I want to lead a unit, because I don't want to manage people," I told Michelle, my own director, when I consulted her. Though I had managed others occasionally and informally as a sales consultant, my full-time job as a project manager involved more than enough management for me; bringing along the projects also meant bringing along the people doing those projects.

Michelle encouraged me. "You never know if it's for you until you try it," she said. "Leading a team of independent consultants is even easier than managing teams at your work, and I'm sure you're great at that." She clearly believed in me when she said, "I know you can do this, and do it well." Michelle's comments, and of course, her compliments, were hard to dispute. Still, deep inside, I had doubts. Intuition warned I should not go forward, this was not the right course for me.

Michelle's confidence stifled those doubts. So did my own sense of myself as loyal and dependable: I did not want to let her down. "Why not go for it?" I asked myself. "It could be the career for me. If I succeed, I can quit my day job." I listened to her confidence, not my own doubts, and went forward. From then on, though those doubts had not really increased, the pressures and frustrations of my day job became unbearable. Soon my second job presented itself as an escape instead of a sideline—"I must become a director. If I don't, I'll be stuck in my 9-to-5."

Qualification, a lengthy, involved, and expensive process, started in October. Four months later, I received a directorship. It felt like a big accomplishment, an honor. Companywide recognition and valuable rewards made me feel like a star.

I'd been good at building customer relationships, and now, as a director, I had good relationships with consultants below me. But those relationships didn't necessarily boost my consultants' sales, nor did I have the authority to evaluate, put on notice, or even fire those who didn't perform, an authority I'd exercised as a call-center manager. Managing sales consultants, especially those who needed help, ate into my own sales. Besides more responsibilities and less time, my own sales targets as a director were far higher.

Within the year, I realized that sales alone were the yardstick now, whether mine or my team's. I saw, too, that I'd never been that good at, or even liked, the sales aspect of this work. As sales figures loomed larger, selling became more difficult. I'd never struggled to meet my targets. I struggled now, which drained my enthusiasm and motivation, never fully mobilized because of those initial doubts.

My sales soon suffered. Eventually, I missed targets routinely. I had no choice but to step down. That was humiliating. I also had to return the rewards, which was even more humiliating. At the same time, though, tremendous relief washed over me. I could finally stop pushing to meet monthly goals. Though I burned with the shame of failure, I also felt free of that constant pressure.

I worked through that episode, as time on my contract ticked down, seeking insight rather than assigning blame. Ready to leave, hoping for new opportunities, I could focus much more clearly on my inner conflict when Michelle urged me to move up—the same conflict disturbing me now, a dissonance that ran deep.

The split wasn't just between one set of competing values, but between a couple of sets. My wish for freedom from managing a team clashed with loyalty to my director. My wish for a steady income and benefits conflicted with my desire to leave my day job, which offered that paycheck and benefits. These conflicts were hard enough to resolve, but a fear-based value also shadowed my choices: becoming a director seemed the only way out of a job I hated.

In the end, my initial, instinctive feeling was accurate: director-ship was not right for me. Everything I did to shut out and ignore that information led me into further difficulty and humiliation. My need to escape my job, which drove me down that byway, also kept me from examining my values or understanding my true path, my purpose in life.

Living boldly, as Marcus Aurelius' words suggest, doesn't mean traveling blind. In the days before radar, sonar, and GPS, travelers steered by the stars. As we shape our own journeys through life, we must find our own stars, take our own path, the one that fits our needs, abilities, and values.

To follow that path and run with those stars, we must know our destination. Our perspectives on life, our beliefs about ourselves, and the things and people most important to us, shape and suggest that destination.

How we reach it, too, arises from who we are, how we see, and what we value. Will we fly, walk, sail, or take the bus? Money buys time, so how important is time? Securing money costs time, so how important is money? Our continuing assessment and reassessment, our willingness to change perspectives when we get new information, lets us look beyond ourselves and see the stars, those eternal, reliable companions and guides.

Our plan, based on what's possible, what we're capable of, what we want or deserve, and what experiences along the way are important to us, presents itself. With that plan we can set off, confident in our arrangements, but also prepared to revise the plan as events unfold. Whether we're traveling abroad or navigating life, this high-level process gives us the perspective, confidence, and flexibility to reach our destination.

Sometimes just getting past that first step—figuring out the destination—seems so difficult that we get stuck. Sometimes, even if we settle on a destination, and even if we overcome fear and doubt to reach it, we question the journey's meaning because the view doesn't seem worth the climb. The effort we made exceeds the satisfaction we find. That was what happened with my directorship. I never wanted to go there again. And it seemed I might not have to.

Just before my contract expired, I attended a management seminar. The speaker introduced herself as a life coach. She said she helped clients see themselves differently. She encouraged them as they discovered lives that suited their abilities, their character, their needs and wants, their natures. Her words rang within me, as deep as those doubts I'd suppressed. I recognized that what she described was what I was meant to do.

The part I liked best about every job I'd ever held was improving people's lives. Helping my project teams rethink their approach to problems satisfied me. Weight Watchers meetings inspired me, and I inspired others. Clients' pleasure during product demonstrations pleased me, too. I took delight in witnessing my colleagues, my classmates, or my clients see themselves in a new, and brighter, light. I enjoyed seeing their energy and confidence soar.

Life coach. This was a profession. I could pursue it. My joy in helping others could become full time, instead of a sideline. Could become the whole job instead of a shining, but unimportant, aspect of meeting others' goals.

The elements now had gathered. I still wasn't ready to watch the stars. Not until the call came from darkness and woke me up.

My contract ended July 31. On August 1, I drove 250 miles in order to care for my mother. She was dying. I wrestled my ambivalence all the way. I was grateful. I wanted to be there for her, to pay her back, if that was even possible, for forty-six years of love and support, for the many blessings I'd received simply by being her daughter. But I was afraid. I didn't want to move back home. I didn't want to watch her become someone I didn't know, someone who would fade away and be gone forever.

She was an amazing woman who grabbed life's brass ring early. Instead of spending her days outside with her friends, she practiced piano for hours. She planned to earn a scholarship and get a college education, something her parents could never afford. Way back in the 1950s, she understood that being a college-educated black woman would give her, and her family, advantages.

She earned a four-year music scholarship. To take advantage of it, she rode the bus back and forth from Philadelphia to her suburban college three hours every day. She graduated and became a teacher.

She loved working with kids, but over the years administrators and school-system bureaucracy wore her down. She wanted the best for her students, but the best wasn't easy, or even possible, sometimes. For what *was* possible, she had to keep on pushing, which was a distraction and an annoyance.

Such conflicts made her job difficult, a difficulty that made her unhappy. I watched as that unhappiness grew. She told me once that she felt stuck. After thirty years, the last fifteen of them unpleasant to miserable, she could retire, free of that constant pressure.

I understood that dissatisfaction, I understood that pressure to meet outside goals. Having seen my mother enjoy a leisurely retirement, I also understood that relief and freedom. But I was too young to give up on finding happiness in my work—retirement was years away. I knew her story, and I wanted to change the ending of mine.

As the miles blurred past, I considered my situation. Things had to change, and those changes had to be major. The life coach's presentation opened a door. It helped me see the crossroads and my path. My next job search wouldn't be a hopeless grind. It wouldn't equip me with a badge I could swipe to check my soul at some corporate door. My next position would finance a career change, and my next position, too, would give me coaching skills.

Despite my ambivalence, despite the situation, I wanted very much to see my mother and spend time with her. That August day, I thought I'd have more of it. Instead, she faded quickly, bedridden and completely dependent on me, my brother, and her live-in aide. My mom and I traded roles. Once, as a young child, I'd been completely dependent on her, but at this point she was completely dependent on me. By the end, she lost her hearing; we had to shout at her, but she couldn't understand. She died twelve days after I got home.

Deeply grateful I'd been able to be with her, and to be her advocate during her last days, I emptied and sold her house. I landed a new job in just three months, a personal record. I also researched coach-training programs, and almost enrolled in one. Settling her affairs, starting the new job, and grieving for her, though, felt like plenty right then.

A year later, I'd gotten comfortable at work. I was good at the job, and I'd found ways to cope with what didn't suit me. Life, having settled into a new normal, almost smothered my plans to be a life coach. An awkward misunderstanding with a coworker brought them sharply to mind again. My boss asked me to map out a process that affected his team but that was under the purview of another department. Objections arose that I was overstepping my bounds. "Back off," was the message, given in a very territorial way.

Life's fleeting nature, too, smacked me upside the head when I learned that Tim, my high-school sweetheart, had died at age forty-nine. I revisited the crossroads I'd reached at the end of the contract. "What are you doing, Patricia?" I asked myself. "Are you settling for a life that doesn't fit your purpose? If so, what are you waiting for?"

Days later, I signed up, without hesitation or regret, for the first round of all-day, intense weekend classes 100 miles away. Rather than worrying about how I might come across or what I should say, I felt excited anticipation. By the second hour of Day One, my classmates and I felt like we'd known each other for years.

Each day began with centering, as you've practiced in these chapters. On Day Two, our classmate Elaine led ours. "Close your eyes," she said. "Picture a river, with its many twists and turns. Imagine that it is twenty years from today, and this river represents your life. The people you've met, the experiences you've had. The decisions you've made." Tears stung my eyes as Elaine painted this picture. I sensed my mom's presence. That sentence from her yearbook floated up: "Life is a river of passing events; swift is its current."

Mommy! She was with me, supporting me, cheering me on, telling me to do more with my life than simply exist. She understood how important it was to free myself from the discomfort, and even pain, of living in ways that didn't fit. I swallowed my tears and centered myself, feeling again that freeing relief: I knew she understood.

At 7 p.m., after the last class, I drove home weary but also elated. My mind raced with thoughts of what life would be like when I was doing what I was meant to do. I was euphoric at the prospect, but also a bit sad and hollow, disappointed that the weekend was over. After the fun of camaraderie, the challenge of learning, the revelations of visioning, I headed to a dark and empty house where no one waited to share all this.

Halfway into the trip, my mother returned to my thoughts, renewing that strong sense of her presence and her encouragement I'd felt on Day Two. I saw my father, too, raising his arm at that last PT session, determined to insist on being himself until the day he died. Comforted, I realized that these important people were still encouraging me. Their love and strength fired my conviction to continue down this path.

Back home, energized but exhausted, I fell into bed, expecting deep sleep. Instead, as I settled myself, tears streamed down my face. A trickle grew to a flood. The outpouring shocked and cleansed me. It seemed to clear my mind. At first I thought I was crying because I couldn't phone my mom and share the weekend's experience with her. That wasn't necessary, I reflected. She'd been there in spirit.

Grief hadn't touched me to tears. Happiness had. The joyful certainty that I finally knew what I was meant to do. That I realized my purpose, which meant I could pursue it. Which meant I could receive its rewards frequently and fully, instead of occasionally and by happenstance.

A purpose is the reason something exists. Our life purpose is the reason each of us is placed on this earth. My purpose, as I came to express it, is "to connect with others on a spiritual level to help them understand and manifest their greatness."

That purpose brought out my passion. Grasping that purpose felt so good, gave me a joy so tremendous, it moved me to tears. It moved me, too, to an eagerness I hadn't felt since childhood: I couldn't wait to help others find their purpose. I was impatient to encourage them to plot their course. To see them run with the stars and feel the joy I felt that moment.

Several months after that, as I continued coach training, I also felt free to pursue things I'd never dreamed of before. I tried on various dreams—traveling; learning a foreign language; becoming a public speaker. I explored the idea of moving to a foreign country.

These inclinations seemed to come out of nowhere. I wondered if I were channeling my parents' hopes and dreams, unlived by them, unknown to me. I cannot say. I can say they passed along their strength. I can say their departure caused me to discover that strength, an imperishable legacy that's helped me Kick-start my own dreams and set my course to run with the stars.

Finding, knowing, and keeping your purpose before you mobilizes your desire to find the path to it, a desire full of hope, confidence, and enthusiasm. Desire is born of purpose and starts us on our path. Those positive feelings put you into positive situations, which in turn improve your life. Your joy spreads to those around you, affecting the world for good. As you become happier, the world's burdens lighten, influencing conditions toward happiness, too.

Life's purpose, as I've suggested, isn't always easy to find. Ascertaining it can be difficult and daunting for several reasons. First, we answer to many values. Finding that one or two that, taken together, fulfill our deepest desires and move us toward our full potential is difficult.

Next, the values we answer to include not only those that are indeed ours and are important to honor, but also values we've adopted or inherited from others, which are not, at their core, truly important to us.

Further, our principles may conflict with each other, creating discord and conflict in ourselves. That conflict gives us difficulty deciding and moving forward, and our energy tumbles, creating a sluggishness and inertia.

Finally, the accumulation of limiting beliefs and other mental blocks blinds us, obscuring all the potential paths we could take following our life's purpose. Is it any wonder so many people struggle to find what they truly want to do in life?

All journeys have purpose and meaning, but experiencing, living in, the purpose and meaning most powerful to us brings abiding joy, peace, and contentment. Immersing ourselves in purpose is what we do when we live boldly. We live deliberately, which means that we live *on* purpose, and we live *with* purpose.

That purpose, our life's purpose, is what fuels our desires, the third catalyst to bold living. The stars of purpose not only help us navigate life with greater ease, they are vital to the bold life we've pondered in these pages. Purpose will take you on your own journey, one in which you will find, rediscover, or refine your understanding of what is most important for you to experience in life.

Now, let's check the alignment of your purpose statement with your true values. As you center, explore, map and claim in this way, you renew and revise your perspective. In life, as in travel, thoughtful planning includes flexibly assessing and reassessing your goals and destination. Do this as often as necessary to home in on what is right for you, given your changing perspectives, your value system, and your situation.

ALIGN WITH THE STARS

<u>CENTERING</u>

- Come to a comfortable seated position.

- Breathe in deeply through your nose for a count of 3.

- Exhale through your nose for a count of 6.

- Close your eyes.

- Breathe in stillness and feel your oneness with your surroundings.

- Relax and be at peace with what is.

- Focus on your breath and let it anchor you to the present moment.

- Breathe and be allowing your body to settle into the peace of the stillness.

- When you feel ready, take in one more deep breath.

- Hold it at the top briefly.

- Slowly exhale and open your eyes.

- You are ready.

<u>EXPLORING</u>

1. Now go back to the exploring you did in the first chapter.
   - Reread your responses, keeping in mind the information in Chapters 3 and 4 about perspective and self-confidence.
   - Read your descriptions aloud.

2. Consider the values you tied to this purpose statement.
   - What are you feeling?

3. List the words that describe your feelings.

- Do these feelings and thoughts suggest conflict or harmony between your value system and this goal?
- What do you see that makes you answer as you do?

MAPPING

1. If in harmony:
    - What emotions stirred up in you?
    - Are they the same or different from those you felt the first time you did the activity?
    - Are they more intense or less intense?
    - What have you learned since you wrote that purpose statement about values, perspective, and self-confidence?
    - How might you use what you've learned to write an even stronger purpose statement?

2. If not in harmony:
    - What emotions stirred up in you?
    - Are they the same or different from those you felt the first time you did the activity?
    - Are they more intense or less intense?
    - Pinpoint the values that contradict or clash with each other.
    - Write them down.
        - » Ask yourself why each is important to you.
        - » Do any arise from your sense of obligation or your need to avoid a negative consequence?
        - » Do two or more values seem equally important, leaving you at an impasse?

» What is causing the disharmony? Write out the source of the disconnect.

CLAIMING

1. Now that you've reassessed, what do you want to do with the purpose statement you wrote earlier?

2. For harmony—if you wish, revise or rewrite your purpose statement. (You may also leave it as it is.)

3. For not in harmony—you may choose to rework or rewrite your purpose statement now or come back to it later, once the dust has settled and the upset of disharmony has cooled.

4. But don't put it off too long. Waiting a few days may yield new perspectives, but waiting a few weeks tends to blur awareness. A strong written purpose statement is the foundation for insight, and for living more boldly.

CENTERING

- With hands open and palms up, close your eyes.
- Breathe in deeply and allow a sense of appreciation to flow through your body. Exhale and say, "Thank you."
- Breathe in gratitude.
- Breathe out and feel the relief that being thankful brings.
- Feel the vibrancy of purpose and meaning all around you.
- Breathe in love.
- Breathe in peace.
- When you are ready, rub your hands together until there is heat.
- Cup them across your eyes, allowing the radiant warmth to fill your

mind. Breathe.

- As you exhale, remove your hands and open your eyes.
    - See your true divinity.
    - Feel your power.
    - Imagine the life you deserve to live.

CHAPTER 6
STEER WITH PURPOSE

When I compare the way I lived and thought before becoming aware of my purpose and values to the way I live and think now, the distance I've traveled and the clarity I've gained still amaze me. Like most people, I started out believing that life is a struggle. That attitude seemed to make it even more of a struggle. The effort to reach goals not my own, and the cost of accepting limits, whether set by others, by situations, or even by myself—was enormous.

I read somewhere that life was never meant to be a struggle. I wanted to believe that, and I set myself to believe it, but I didn't really know from experience whether it was true. To learn, I had to search my soul and examine my life. "The unexamined life is not worth living," Socrates said long ago, but that examination takes effort and courage.

As Thoreau noted centuries later, when he wrote that "the mass of men lead lives of quiet desperation," most people can't make that effort and don't have that courage. Deep into my own quiet desperation, I began questioning the accuracy of that warlike idea of life as struggle. I began to ask myself what ruled me. Duty? Pleasure? Work? Self? Breadth? Depth? Head? Heart?

I had to search my soul and change my perspective. Doing so was often a struggle, but as I acquired those habits, life itself, astonishingly, came to involve much less struggle—and much more satisfaction.

Values drive us all, but we are often unaware of how powerfully our values, like our limitations and blindnesses, work in the background. They often conflict. Remaining unaware of them and their oppositions can mean that we honor things that aren't really important, as when I put loyalty to Michelle over my reluctance to manage others. Being able to see the interplay of values, to know if we're acting on a value born of passion or fear, lets us move forward with authenticity, confidence, and purpose.

When we pause to examine and articulate our values, to revisit or revise our purpose statement, when we draw on those documents during uncertainty, we provide ourselves with a sense of security and grant ourselves an authority that lets us act boldly, free of fear. Our values reveal our purpose, and our purpose, in turn, anchors us to our values. These are our guides; they ignite the burning desire that moves and focuses our journey.

Setting meaningful goals, which results in this desire, is just as important as the other two. Purpose, once discerned, also generates desire, which carries us forward on our journey. Discovering purpose, though it is the first task before setting off, is not something done once and dismissed. Without the combination of reason (which helps us shift perspective) and desire (which propels us), without a willingness to reassess and revise our purpose and our strategies, our dreams can fade, our desires wane.

Revisiting our purpose, checking, or even changing, our reason for being, is necessary often along the way. Examining our values reveals our purpose. Seeking our purpose lets us uncover our desires. Following our desires moves us to achieve our purpose. Attaining our purpose adds to our zest for life, bringing us joy, peace, and a sense of calm, even when chaos seems to reign.

Bear in mind, though, that the challenges don't end. Knowing your purpose and running with the stars clarifies your situation, and helps you set meaningful goals. But it's not always easy to stay focused and maintain your perspective. Even when you've opened yourself to working with the three catalysts, life, that strong current, still offers surprises, wake-up calls, and moments that get you into deep (or hot) water.

STAY THE COURSE

Divorced three years, I'd dated sporadically, though I'd met no one who might interest me for the long term. Considering prospective partners was easier, because, I believed, I'd grown to know myself better and I understood what was necessary in my personal life, and what was negotiable.

I'd joined a local hiking group so I could meet new people while staying in shape. They'd invited me to their holiday party, and I decided to go. The Christmas party was festive, but as one of the newest members, I didn't know many guests. The tree was fragrant, the decorations bright enough to spark my holiday mood and keep me circulating. At the end of an hour, though, I was ready to call it a night.

That's when Jerry appeared. A tall man with chestnut brown skin and light caramel eyes, he smiled warmly. In a low, husky voice that caught my attention, he told me his name and asked, "Have you been a River City Hiker long?"

Returning his smile, I introduced myself. "I joined two months ago," I added. "I've lived in the city for years, but I wanted to expand my horizons and meet new people."

"I've been a member for a year and a half, but I've only gone on four hikes," he said, a bit guiltily. He looked away, considering what to say next. "I'm going to be more active this coming year," he said, apparently assuring himself of this as well as me. He was clearly shy and a bit nervous about making the first move, but after breaking the ice he was more confident.

I wasn't immediately attracted to him. Despite his height, he slouched, as if concealing his prominent paunch, and his hairline was receding. But he was sincere and intelligent, and he'd had the courage to start a conversation. "I'm fairly new to town, transferred in for a job two years ago. I joined to meet new people, too," he added. He hesitated. "And to shave my waistline a bit." He smiled and patted his stomach.

He intrigued me because he was bold enough to open a conversation and because he was bold enough to poke fun at himself. Both took confidence. Jerry brought us both eggnogs and we moved on to discussing music. "You're kidding!" he said. "I was in marching band, too. I played the trumpet." He moved closer, smiling still more broadly. "But what I love is classical guitar. I bought a guitar a few months ago and I'm learning to play."

"I've toyed for the last few years with dusting off my flute," I said, "but I haven't brought myself to do it. I guess I'm afraid to find out how much I've forgotten and how bad I'll sound," I admitted. We both chuckled.

"Music makes me feel like, like—" He closed his eyes, searching for words. "Like even when things aren't right, they can be."

I saw something beautiful in Jerry then, someone who could go deep and be vulnerable. "Maybe I wrote him off too fast," I said to myself. "Maybe he is the one."

Our first date was for coffee. We moved on to discussing the arts and our hobbies. "In high school, I worked on the set crew for 'Romeo and Juliet.' Building everything was fun," he said, remembering. "I wish I could do that now," he added, looking away. The guilt I'd caught at the Christmas party resurfaced.

Trying to lift the energy, I said, "There are all kinds of local theater groups here, maybe you could help them out."

"I guess I could," he said noncommittally. "Mm-hm." Something painful there.

Leaving this obviously sore subject, I said, "*The Lion King* is coming to town. Have you ever seen that?" Our conversation continued easy and agreeable from there, but I noticed that he ended his sentences as if asking a question instead of making a statement. The confidence Jerry showed at the party had faded, while the social awkwardness increased.

That mm-hm, or a nervous laugh, sometimes punctuated his comments, too. Occasionally he muttered to himself almost inaudibly, "I shouldn't have said that." Somehow I had reservations; Jerry might not be the one for me. I genuinely liked him, though, and he offered many of the qualities I sought in a partner. He loved music, enjoyed the theater, and was considerate in every way.

The depth I'd seen at the Christmas party convinced me to give him the benefit of the doubt—his awkwardness might simply mean he was an introvert, like me, not that he was down on himself. If that were so, he wouldn't have had the nerve even to ask me out. Right?

Our second, more committed, date was for dinner and a movie. We saw a romantic comedy, *The Hundred-Foot Journey*, and went to a casual seafood restaurant. On our third date, we went to see *Long Day's Journey into Night*. Dinner followed at the Down Home, a restaurant offering Southern comfort food. We discussed O'Neill's play over drinks, and of course that discussion, about the unhealed wounds of a New England family, and their sins, destined to be repeated, led naturally to discussing our own families. The food, the ambience, and the wine with dinner made that conversation open and easy.

"Did you spend Christmas in Maryland with your parents?"

I asked.

"No, not this year," he said quickly, pondering his plateful of chicken and waffles. "I haven't done that for a few years now. They've got their own thing going on. This year they went to New York City," he explained, looking up at me to show he was OK with it. But I sensed there was more to it.

"Last year I went to the beach for Christmas," I said. I swallowed my sadness. "I didn't want to wake up at my house alone on Christmas morning. I always spent it at Mommy's." I fell silent, working to hold back tears. "This year, though, I stayed at my house. It really wasn't too bad." I forced myself to smile. He was lucky—he could spend Christmas with his parents. How foolish not to. I let my annoyance pass and did not pry; he had his reasons. If we continued dating, I'd learn them soon enough.

Dinner continued. I learned that Jerry was an animal lover, and that his cat, Simone, had passed six months before. "A house just doesn't seem quite complete without a cat, does it?" I asked. "My cat, Tabitha, died about a year ago."

Our conversation meandered from pets to our mutual lack of interest in sports and our dreams of travel. We seemed to have enough in common, and we enjoyed each other's company. We started seeing each other on weekends. We always did things I enjoyed, things I'd done by myself, usually, since my divorce. It was nice not to go alone, nice to discuss the play or movie we'd just seen.

The dates were lovely, but after three months, the silence in between them began to bother me. We'd spend a wonderful

Saturday evening or Sunday afternoon together, then I'd hear nothing for a week, even two. Sometimes I called Jerry to chat, but he never called me. The phone works in both directions, I thought, growing annoyed.

"Could you call between dates?" I asked.

"You know, I've felt a bit disconnected, myself," he answered. "Sure, I'll call during the week to see how you are." Relieved that my request didn't seem unusual, I was happy to hear that.

The silences continued as before, however. I felt, somehow, like The Other Woman, the one he saw when his main squeeze was out of town. Now the pain of conflicting values sharpened. Feeling connected in a relationship was important to me, but not being alone was, too.

Still, when we saw each other, Jerry brought me presents—flowers, loose tea, and other things he knew I liked—out of the blue and for no reason. At dinner, he shyly showed his desire by reaching across the table to take my hand. Occasional moments of deep conversation gave me further glimpses into his soul. All these were things I'd never experienced in a relationship. I didn't know how much I treasured these little gestures until Jerry made them.

Besides all that, Jerry was smart. He had a good sense of humor. He seemed romantic, and he enjoyed the arts. He had a good job and plenty of money. So, despite the fact that he wasn't attentive when we weren't together, and might even be emotionally unavailable, I looked the other way. Maybe he would change. Maybe he would call, as we discussed and as he agreed to. Maybe—

That winter was particularly cold and snowy. Spring took her slow time arriving. My joy in the long-delayed daffodils, my anticipation of milder weather and going out more, fought with a shadowy feeling that I'd sold out, that I'd accepted Jerry, but that he was not right for me. A feeling that I'd been untrue—not to him, but to myself.

Months passed, then it was May. I was still fighting those inner doubts, still working to convince myself that Jerry was the one. It was harder work by then. I knew by then that I'd settled. That Jerry was not, and probably never would be, deeply involved with me. I had a man, he cared for me, yet I was unhappy. He could not do this one simple thing: call between dates. I wasn't asking much, but clearly it was too much. His unwillingness after repeated requests, and despite giving his word, fed undercurrents of unease that chilled and shadowed what I wanted in my life.

Just a few months of this frayed me emotionally and picked at my confidence, causing me sometimes to question my own worth and doubt whether Jerry was even attracted to me. Thoughts of how to approach the problem consumed me each week as I awaited, but never received, those promised calls. Finally, he sent this text message: "Hey, just checking in." That was it. No call. No question about when he should call.

I sat myself down and examined the situation. *What the hell are you doing, Patricia?* came the question, a question that cut through my loneliness-driven need not to be alone, even if it meant spending time with someone who only *almost* fit the bill. A question that changed my perspective and made me say, finally, "Enough."

I'd cut Jerry too much slack. Giving him the benefit of the doubt over and over, playing second fiddle to whatever— or whoever—else occupied his time increased the doubt and undercut even the good things in this friendship. It was painfully hard not to judge myself, bitterly hard to face how strong a force my fear of loneliness really was. I took consolation in knowing that my own question woke me up, not some outside event or emotional disaster.

"Jerry," I said slowly, when he called to arrange our next date, "let's not go out tomorrow." Despite my wish not to hurt his feelings, irritation rose in my voice.

"What? Why not?" He seemed perplexed.

"I'm tired of this. We see each other on weekends, and we have a great time. You take me nice places, we do fun things. We have deep conversations. But I don't hear from you again until our next date. I've asked if you'd call during the week, even just to check in. You agree. But then you don't call. I'm tired of waiting for a call that never comes," I said, the fullness of my anger breaking through.

Silence. Jerry finally spoke, his voice as low as if I'd punched him. He seemed surprised that I wanted to end things, bewildered that after six months I wanted more than a text message. "I'm just not ready for that." His voice louder, more indignant, he added, "And I won't let you push me into doing something I'm not ready for."

"It doesn't seem that much to ask—"

"Fine!" he said. He hung up, leaving me stunned. How swiftly it was over. How willing he was to let go of our six months together. He didn't try to hang on. He didn't offer to change his ways. I wouldn't have been able to believe he could, anyway.

I'd spent precious time and energy on a relationship that wasn't right for me. Even though my gut had told me this all along, my fear of being alone overrode that truth. I'd invested months with Jerry, but I'd felt alone anyway. My intuition spoke. Not listening harmed even the good parts—I wished so hard for a future, I had trouble enjoying the present.

Here, too, the obstacle opened onto the path. Once I asked the question, the insoluble problem of an unrewarding friendship, as well as the loneliness that prolonged it, and distorted my under-standing, and my actions, came into clearer focus—and revealed my next step.

Though it took time and effort to forgive myself for waiting so long to examine the values at cross-purposes here, I survived mostly unscathed. The information and growth this relationship offered caused me to reflect and revise. I could let Jerry go and wish him well. Even though we didn't stay together, ending our connection seemed to offer Jerry, too, a chance to reflect and even to change. I hope he, too, grew. Though all this was years ago, it is a valuable reminder of how difficult keeping perspective can be.

Much farther down the path, with that experience, and the others I've examined, including the directorship, I now knew far more about what was truly important, and understood, too, those aspects of life on which I couldn't compromise—even with myself. When my parents passed on, however, I worried that I might not be able to do without their advice and emotional support.

Despite my misgivings, and my feeling that I now had to navigate life as an orphan, I became more aware than ever of how much my parents gave me, resources of confidence and strength that I tapped every day. During the 365 days following my mother's death, I not only survived, I thrived, summoning the energy and industry to clean out and sell my childhood home and to secure a new job. In addition, I overcame early challenges at the new job in an inventive way that helped my reputation and career.

The company hired me for my expertise in devising novel approaches to managing projects. At first, after project sponsors assigned me to several that had run aground, they asked for but didn't heed my advice. A territorial, rather than a collegial, attitude, permeated the company, hampering communications, causing emergencies, and setting these projects, now mine, up to fail. The blame would fall right on my shoulders. To keep my job, I'd have to get cooperation fast.

I found a paradoxical way to turn the situation around, selling my solutions as probable failures while appealing to the sponsors' desire to seem open-minded. When they said, "That would never work," I answered, "You know, you're probably right. But don't you think we owe it to the company to try it and be sure? The up-side is, this approach could salvage our project."

Unwilling to appear inflexible, or unwilling to appear to put their egos ahead of the organization, they tried my approach. They soon saw its benefits and noticed how it turned the grounded projects around. My credibility soared. My company soon saw me as a valuable asset.

My parents' deaths, and my own experiences, yielded new perspectives that helped me see challenges as opportunities rather than obstacles. That understanding revolutionized my approach to rescuing the projects. It moved me forward in other areas, too. On a personal level, after many years' silence, I began writing again. I enrolled in creative writing classes, amassing quite a portfolio of work. I even created a blog, on which I post regularly. In addition, I've maintained my target weight, and, having taken up karate, I earned my purple belt.

Almost exactly two years after my mother's death, as I evaluated my situation, I realized that although my parents were no longer with me on earth, they had instilled in me (and I had learned) everything I needed. I was already on the journey after they passed. I'd already found my purpose within that first year.

They gave me the strength, the courage, and the drive to persevere despite adversity. These gifts were my foundation as I committed to living a bold life, one that my parents would have been proud and happy to watch me live. This means I don't hang back from pursuing my dreams. I continue to learn and to grow and to be.

I become the best Patricia I can, in whatever area I choose, rather than trying to be a good imitation of someone else. I am compassionate and generous. I help others to be the best they can be, too. I take on challenges and give them my all.

In these ways I repay my parents for their sacrifices, the efforts they made so that I could have the best life possible. This value, respect, is important to me. A stranger might make the mistake of thinking I've based my actions on what my parents would want me to do. But it's not just respect for them. The truth is that I respect myself, too, and therefore, I choose freely, undertaking the projects and quests that speak to me, that expand my horizons, or that are important to me and support my purpose.

My values and my parents' values intersect in the way I go about accomplishing my goals and living my purpose—with integrity and authenticity, working always for excellence. This approach honors not only my values but my parents' legacy in me. Integrity and authenticity are essential to the bold life. They light our course; they are the stars with which we run.

As I have continued, my efforts to fulfill my purpose have been increasingly successful. Living this way makes real every day my respect and gratitude for what they gave me. Doing what I desire in a manner that would make them proud is not only my gift back to them, it is the power that fuels my progress and helps me live out my purpose—and live it out boldly.

Now you know how the three catalysts—shifting perspective, building self-confidence, and setting meaningful goals—have helped me live deliberately and boldly, and you've already considered how they can do the same for you.

You've explored, mapped, and claimed your situation, your life, and your values, recording these as guides for your own journey. You've already begun shifting perspective on the world around you, and on yourself. Your values, what you consider truly important, and what kind of life will accommodate those values and needs, are clearer. You may even be so inspired that you've already started making changes.

Now what?

If you're like me, right after reading thought-provoking books or taking workshops, you're afire to implement new ideas. As time passes, though, their sheen fades, and sometimes, so do enthusiasm and investment. Now I want to suggest ways to keep what you've learned in mind, to help you form new habits, and to shelter and maintain your burning desire.

To persevere in living a bold life, you must continue to feel the excitement of new possibilities. You must plant the habit in your consciousness of stopping and seeing things differently. Tried-and-true ways to stay positive, to grow continuously, and to organize time can help you stay motivated when distractions or challenges try to take you off point. They can help you continue boldly, even when life's routines and dramas vie for attention. It is easier to work toward your dreams when you're already moving than to start over from a standstill.

STAY POSITIVE

1. **Find Positive People**

   Surround yourself with positive people. Making your way from the swamp of stuckness, with its lower energy and draining doubts, to higher ground and a more constructive, optimistic perspective is challenging. The challenge is particularly sharp at the start. If others in your world constantly complain and judge, casting dark clouds of negativity over you, your desire can chill, your progress can slow. Seek instead others on the move, those whose bright energy reflects your own, and who pursue their own meaningful goals and live their own purpose. Energy is contagious: which kind do you want to catch?

2. **Return to Center**

   When stressful situations or draining companions exhaust you, pay attention. If your energy falls enough to awaken anxiety, irritation, fear, or worry, center yourself. Take three energy-boosting, cleansing breaths, and return to your living body, your beating heart, your alive-ness—and yourself. Do this as needed to maintain perspective and renew energy. Centering reminds us who we are. It is essential when we examine our situations and reframe our perspectives. It can help us focus, too, on particular areas—summoning courage, for example, or opening ourselves to creativity or gratitude. (To explore additional centering techniques, see Appendix 4)

3. **Include Daily Morning Time**

   Set up your morning ritual, a routine you follow faithfully to ground yourself and remain positive. You might, for example, center yourself and perform a morning meditation. You might write out and read aloud a daily affirmation. You might recite devotional prayers. Your morning ritual is a daily gift you offer yourself and your purpose. This small but powerful interval can light your way and ease your passage, sending you off in fair weather. Time for yourself, and with yourself, raises your energy and helps you find those stars.

4. **Get Moving**

Our bodies are also ourselves. Becoming and staying physically active not only makes moving forward real, it boosts mood, generating endorphins, the feel good-hormones. Daily exercise, especially in the morning, provides another kind of accomplishment, and increases energy and stamina, improving our outlook on the day.

5. **Eat Healthfully**

Eating wisely also boosts positive energy. Our bodies need fuel to work, and we need strength and vigor to live boldly. Foods full of sugars, caffeine, or additives, foods fried, salted, or overloaded with calories don't just harm long-term health, they make us sluggish and tax our metabolism, sometimes even injuring or inflaming our systems. Nutritious and wholesome food, lightly prepared, helps keep us feeling well physically, which contributes tremendously to feeling well mentally and emotionally.

6. **Sleep Enough**

Rest keeps us physically, mentally, and emotionally at the top of our game. Inadequate sleep impairs thinking and judgment, makes us irritable or depressed, and exacerbates a host of chronic medical problems from stiff joints to high blood pressure. Sleep, like food, restores and recharges us, and is just as essential.

CONTINUE GROWING

1. **Turn Challenges to Opportunities**

   Identify a challenge, an aspect of your life that holds you back. Reframe it as an opening rather than an obstacle or failure. Create a plan to improve it. Perhaps your busy schedule interferes with mindfulness. Possibly you've considered finances, health, or education roadblocks in the past. Or a relationship has you feeling trapped or abandoned.

   Evaluate your challenge as if you were meeting it for the first time. Center yourself and do as we've practiced, exploring in writing what practical plan you might make to overcome it, what actions and attitudes that plan requires, and what successes you've had in the past that might help you find the assurance to follow this plan, acting to conquer this challenge. Write out your actions, and your successes. Revise them, and the plan, as needed.

2. **Track the Negative**

   To fall back into judging ourselves or others narrows our vision and limits our perception. If this attitude is darkening your days, make a notebook into a judgment journal. As judgmental thoughts cross your mind, record how much time you gave them and make a checkmark. Doing this daily for a week will show exactly how much time you spend in that negative way. Noticing how often these thoughts occur is the first step toward breaking this destructive habit, because it helps you stop those draining thoughts before they distract you from more positive considerations. This practice is also useful if you get caught in other kinds of negative, repetitive thinking, like worry, self-doubt, or fear.

3. **Read or Listen**

   Another way to expand your view and change your thinking is to explore a range of personal-development books. These are available as e-books and audiobooks, as well as in print. Most local libraries stock all formats free for download or checkout, so you need not break the bank to widen your horizons.

4. **Revisit *Growing Bold***

   Add a reminder on your calendar to reread a chapter from this book once a month as a refresher. Each time we read or hear information, we receive it differently because we are different. We've embarked on or undergone new experiences, we may have discarded or discovered insights or beliefs, or we may simply be more rested and receptive.

5. **Work with a Life Coach**

   Life coaches are professionals. They can help you see the forest—looking at your life, identifying your next step. They can help you see the trees—clarifying your goals, planning ways to reach them. Life coaches can keep you focused by helping you stay accountable. They can work with you to examine where you're blocked and help you get unstuck. Some coaches specialize in certain areas, like retirement, divorce, job seeking.

Their open and nonjudgmental approach helps reveal clients' highest values and goals. Their encouragement and understanding, as well as the trustworthy atmosphere they provide, can offer the extra strength you need to unstick yourself and achieve your goals.

MANAGE TIME

1. **Make Room for What's Valuable**

   Sometimes we discourage ourselves from setting new goals because it seems we have no more space in our busy schedules. All that work and thought you've put into exploring, mapping, and claiming here, as well as your own inward discussion with yourself about values, has probably showed you more clearly what's most important. Even so, you may feel that you don't have time to act on your insights.

   Your notebook can help inventory the days, analyze how you spend them, and show where your time goes. You might discover that you spend a surprising number of hours watching TV, surfing the Internet, or talking on the phone. You might discover that you can save time in little ways by becoming more efficient or by jettisoning tasks or attitudes you accepted without question. You might rise earlier or retire later, spending this found time working toward your goals, seeking what you value. When you realize and claim what is truly important, your confidence and desire will rise, and you will find even more time.

2. **Plan Actions with Deadlines**

   Revisit your work in Chapters 1 and 2, thinking more deeply about your goals, your purpose, and your criteria for success. Break down your criteria into specific components, let's call them buckets.

   If my goal is to straighten my office within thirty days, for example, success means that I'll have no papers on my desk at night except in the In and Out bins, and that my file drawers will be alphabetized and hold active clients' files only. The components of success, therefore, my two buckets of work, will be "develop process for clearing desk" and "purge and organize file drawers."

   I'd use buckets small enough to finish in no more than a month, listing under each the steps required to finish. I'd sequence the steps logically, setting deadlines for each task that let me finish in thirty days. If your buckets take longer than a month, try breaking them into components that fit into thirty days. This way you'll see progress right away and won't feel overwhelmed.

3. **Work Backward from Milestones**

   For bigger goals that we want to finish months in the future, it helps to work backward from the expected date we reach the big goal. First we decide what buckets of work—which milestones—we must complete, and when. For example, if your big goal is to sell your house in six months, write out which bucket of work (milestone) you'll need to finish each month leading up to Month Six. That's the map; use it to chart a timeline that keeps you focused. Tack that timeline where you can see it to remind you where you're going.

4. **List Weekly and Daily Tasks**

   That timeline also generates tasks large and small. Most goals require interlocking sets of tasks. Some must happen before others, and some are more urgent than others. If I want to organize my vacation snapshots, for example, I have to make or buy a scrapbook. I can do that any time. I have to start by taking photos, though, and I must also choose among them.

   Like those goal buckets, weekly and daily lists ought to be few enough to finish in a limited time. My own daily list includes no more than six tasks, ranked by priority. *A*-tasks must get done today, *B*-tasks are next most pressing, and should be done today if possible, and *C*-tasks would be nice to finish today but aren't pressing. Creating weekly lists on Sundays and daily lists the night before lets us get going on them every morning without having to figure out where to start.

5. **Chart Progress**

   Picture your progress. A pie chart or bar chart, or even a graph that looks like a thermometer, can show headway toward each goal. If the goal is six months away, divide the pie or thermometer into sixths and shade in while finishing tasks for a given month. Visual evidence of how things are going focuses your efforts.

6. **Revisit Goals Daily**

   Whatever we focus on manifests in our lives. As part of your daily morning ritual, rewrite the goals you're working toward. Doing so reminds you of your destination, keeping a sharp and lasting focus on it.

7. **Reset Misses**

When you set deadlines and miss, resist judgment and negative feelings. Don't give up on the goal, simply reshape your path toward it. A missed deadline signals delay, not defeat—giving up doesn't nourish dreams or a bold life. The delay may indeed raise our confidence about moving forward, because a miss makes us reassess.

We move back the deadline, we don't discard the goal. We analyze how far we came to see how far we must go, and we consider how long it took already to calculate how much longer it will take to reach the goal, factoring in everything we learned along the way.

BOLDNESS BY DEGREE

Living more boldly has taught me much. Writing this book has taught me, too, refining my perspective on the world and on myself. Just as writing down experiences, insights, and new perspectives has clarified them for you, writing this has shown me even more about what growing bold really means, and what life lived boldly can offer.

I have come to realize, too, that there are degrees of boldness. When you learn to see new possibilities, when you trust—because you have done the inner work and truly know yourself on a whole new level—that you are capable, you've taken the first giant steps to growing bold.

These actions, this process, helps you leave your comfort zone despite being anxious or even scared. This point of departure, a movement within you, presents your life not as a half-empty glass, but as a half-full, or even an overflowing one.

I didn't set out to grow bold on purpose. I didn't realize that the three catalysts we've now discussed helped me find my path. I bumbled along, encountering them by accident. They presented themselves after the first giant steps I unwittingly took. Perspective shifting, goal setting, and confidence building lit my path as I pursued the inner work, nourishing and also fostering change, choice, and boldness.

As the process continued, other positive qualities arose, including keener self-awareness, higher self-esteem, increased self-discipline, clarity of mind, and creativity, and an inner sense of authenticity and peace. These are the foundation for my next stage of bold living—growing bolder.

People at this stage move easily out of their comfort zones, feeling little, if any, fear, and much more certainty. They know that their results will be good, because they understand that opportunity is everywhere, even in challenges and losses, even in events that most people consider major problems.

At this level, the glass is not only completely full, it never empties. At this level, goals are audacious. Observers might call these goals risky and even foolish. Mohandas Gandhi and Martin Luther King sought such goals. So did Henry Ford and Thomas Edison. So did Jane Addams and Sojourner Truth. So did Helen Keller and Franklin Roosevelt. So did Susan B. Anthony and Ida B. Wells. So did Charles R. Drew and Jonas Salk. These bold souls' apparently risky and foolish goals were intrinsic to their lives and fundamental to their purpose. They achieved them, advancing human understanding in the process.

Self-awareness, self-esteem, self-discipline, clarity of mind, creativity, authenticity, and inner peace are powerful. Each deserves its own chapter. Each, as it grew, strengthened me and sharpened my appetite for adventure. To recount all the places they've led me would need another book. I mention them here to help you understand that your own bold life, too, will rise along a continuum.

The final step brings complete fearlessness. People at this level have no comfort zone to step out of because they routinely take risks. Delighting in the unknown and believing deeply in the perfection in all things, they shrug off the constraints of a comfort zone, of any boundary. Risk is no longer risk to them, because to them the fear of loss that keeps most people from taking a chance seems as unreal as freedom and purpose were to me when I began.

I am not there yet, but I am on the path. And so are you. I wrote this book to show you that. My purpose, and my passion, is to inspire and encourage people to achieve their dreams. I am happiest helping others increase their energy and shift their perception, discovering their lives' true potential. That charged silence as people remember who they are renews my own commitment. That radiant moment when they see at last what they can truly accomplish lights my own way.

Now I can exhale, having shared my path with you, hopeful that the events and insights I've recounted move you to seek your freedom, too, despite your fears. What you've read and written started that process. May you continue it, moving forward with confidence to reap rich possibilities.

Thank you for participating. I wish you, now and in the future, the bravery and perseverance to discover your own purpose and to embark on your own satisfying, exciting, and bold life.

APPENDIXES

APPENDIX 1: THE THREE CATALYSTS

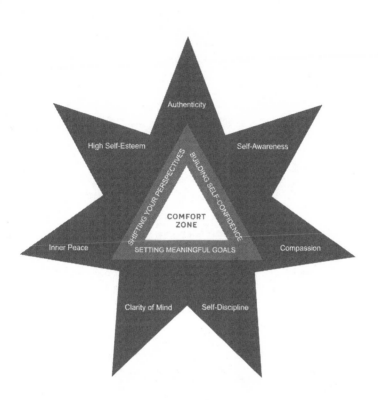

APPENDIX 2: EXPLORING, MAPPING, CLAIMING

1. Always center before starting. This clears your mind so that you can tap into your inner knowing. (See Appendix 4 for a selection of approaches.)

2. Allow yourself time and privacy. Some of the activities will take longer to complete than others. Take the time you need.

3. As you think through and write out your answers, deliberately avoid judging yourself, your past actions, or anything. Stay present to the questions and your answers. If judgmental thoughts or worries start to catch you, take three deep and cleansing breaths and reclaim your focus.

4. Be as open and honest as possible with yourself. Greater honesty brings more clarity. More clarity brings deeper understanding, and more profound results. Take your time, be thoughtful, write out your answers, and enjoy the process.

APPENDIX 3: VALUES

VALUE	VALUE	VALUE
Accomplishment	Friendship	Privacy
Abundance	Fulfillment	Professionalism
Achievement	Fun	Recognition
Adventure	Holistic Living	Respect
Altruism	Honesty	Romance
Autonomy	Humor	Security
Beauty	Integrity	Self-Care
Clarity	Intimacy	Self-Expression
Commitment	Joy	Self-Mastery
Communication	Leadership	Self-Realization
Community	Loyalty	Sensuality
Connecting to others	Nature	Service
Creativity	Openness	Simplicity of Life
Emotional Health	Orderliness	Spirituality
Environment	Peace	Trust
Excellence	Personal Growth	Truth
Family	Partnership	Vitality
Flexibility	Physical Appearance	Walking the Talk
Freedom	Power	Other

APPENDIX 4: CENTERING

INVOKE THE LIFE FORCE

- Close your eyes in order to be with yourself without distraction.
- Get into a comfortable position.
- Breathe in through your nose for a count of 3, and out for a count of 6.
- Take a few breaths and focus on relaxing your body.
- Stay focused on your breath.
- Notice how your shoulders loosen as you exhale.
- Breathe in the brisk cool air of pure light. This is life force.
- Breathe out the gray heavy cloud of tension.
- Focus on your breathing and allow your body to relax.
    - Release your shoulders.
    - Release your arms.
    - Release your torso.
    - Release your legs.
    - Release your feet.
- Be with yourself in this stillness.
- Breathe in energy. Breathe out anxiety.
- Breathe in stillness. Breathe out whatever overwhelms you.
- Continue breathing naturally as long as you'd like.
- Let the wave of relaxation infuse your entire body.
- When you feel ready, take one last deep breath.
- On the exhale, slowly open your eyes.

INVOKE ABUNDANCE

- Seat yourself comfortably.
- Open your hands with palms facing up.
- Close your eyes.
- Breathe in through your nose for a count of 3, and out for a count of 6.
- As you repeat this breathing pattern, notice areas of tightness in your body.
- Let the tension melt away.
- Relax.
- Prepare yourself to receive all the gifts the universe has to offer you.
- Smile as you breathe in your gifts.
- Exhale with appreciation for all that you receive.
- Remain aware that you need not see or know what these gifts are, you must merely be open and receive.
- Continue to smile as you breathe in your gifts.
- Exhale with appreciation.
- Acknowledge your joy.
- Continue breathing, receiving, and appreciating as long as you like.
- When you feel ready, take one last deep breath, and say to yourself "Abundance."
- Open your eyes slowly and exhale.

INVOKE DESTINY

- Seat yourself comfortably.
- Close your eyes.
- Breathe in deeply through your nose for a count of 3, and out for a count of 6.

- As you breathe, let your entire body relax.
- Say to yourself, "There is no right or wrong. It just is."
- Breathe in vitality.
- Breathe out constriction.
- Breathe and allow the spirit inside you to be free.
- Enjoy the energy you receive for as long as you like.
- When you are ready, breathe in deeply one more time.
- As you exhale, say to yourself, "I am the author of my story. I am the master of my destiny."
- Open your eyes.

INVOKE THE CREATIVE

- Seat yourself comfortably.
- Close your eyes.
- Breathe in deeply through your nose for a count of 3, and out for a count of 6.
- As you inhale, breathe in positive energy, saying, "I am a positive light force."
- As you breathe out, expel excuses, saying, "I release the energy within that blocks me."
- Breathe in love.
- Breathe out fear.
- Breathe and embody the positive energy that you are.
- When you are ready, breathe in deeply one more time and say," I am creative."
- As you exhale, say, "I unleash my creativity and it surrounds me."

INVOKE DIVINITY

- Seat yourself comfortably.

- Close your eyes.

- Breathe in deeply through your nose for a count of 3, and out for a count of 6.

- Breathe in cool, brisk air.

- As you exhale, notice how refreshed you feel.

- Bask in knowing that you are a divine being with endless things to offer.

- Breathe in abundant life.

- Breathe out doubt.

- Know that you are divine.

- Be silent and present with yourself.

- Simply breathe and feel refreshed.

- When you are ready, take in one last deep breath.

- As you exhale, say, "I am passion. I am purpose. I am divine."

- Open your eyes slowly.

INVOKE COURAGE

- Seat yourself comfortably.

- Close your eyes.

- Breathe in deeply through your nose for a count of 3, and out for a count of 6. Notice the sensations you feel in your body.

- Pay attention to movements of light that permeate your eyelids.

- Become aware of any sounds and allow them to pass through you like a cloud.

- Breathe in compassion.

- Breathe out blame.

- Breathe in strength.
- Breathe out limitations.
- Open your eyes, preparing to explore, claim, and map.
- Take one more deep breath, and say, "I am Strength, I am Resilience, I am Courage."

INVOKE PRESENCE

- Seat yourself comfortably.
- Breathe in deeply through your nose for a count of 3, and out for a count of 6.
- Close your eyes.
- Breathe in stillness, and feel your oneness with your surroundings.
- Relax and be at peace with what is.
- Focus on your breath and let it anchor you to the present moment.
- Breathe and be, letting your body settle into the peace of the stillness.
- When you feel ready, take one more deep breath.
- Hold that breath briefly at the top.
- Exhale slowly.
- Open your eyes.

BIBLIOGRAPHY

Some books that you may find helpful on your journey into boldness:

Andersen, U. S. *The Magic in Your Mind*. Important Books, 2012.
  Discusses the hidden power of thoughts. Presents ways to tap into the
  secret self below the surface, and to discover a life filled with meaning
  and flow.

Anderson, Erika. *Be Bad First: Get Good at Things Fast to Stay Ready for the
  Future*. New York: Bibliomotion, 2016.
  A deeper look into one aspect of gaining courage; the author outlines
  a four-part strategy she calls ANEW, including exercises to try.

Carlson, Richard, Ph.D. *Don't Sweat the Small Stuff . . . and it's all small stuff:
  Simple Ways to Keep the Little Things from Taking Over Your Life*. New
  York: Hyperion, 1997.
  Carlson's 100 tips for living a more stress-free and enjoyable life offer
  wonderful ways to shift perspective and find the inner sense of calm
  that leads to clarity and unexpected options.

Carter-Scott, Chérie, Ph.D. *If Success is a Game, These are the Rules: Ten Rules
  for a Fulfilling Life*. New York: Broadway Books, 2000.
  Insightful, thorough, and readable, this book includes practical exercises,
  questions to ponder, and strategies to deal with the change success
  brings.

Godin, Seth. *Linchpin: Are you Indispensable?* New York: Portfolio, 2010.

Perceptive and informative explanation of the current state of the economy. Uses wonderful examples to show how to move from being a passionless, indoctrinated cog in the wheel to the kind of leader who holds things together, creates connection with others, and instills purpose in them.

Johnson, Spencer, M.D. *"Yes" or "No": The Guide to Better Decisions.* New York: HarperCollins, 1992.

A parable about the ways in which awareness of our own values and beliefs, challenges to the common viewpoint, and the use of intuition help improve decisions. Making more confident decisions lessens chances of getting stuck.

Ruiz, Don Miguel. *The Four Agreements: A Practical Guide to Personal Freedom.* San Rafael, California: Amber-Allen Publishing, 1997.

Ruiz discusses four practical commitments to change thinking and improve the quality of life, noting how conformity causes people to lose their way. Questioning long-held beliefs and adopting what he calls the Four Agreements—keep your word, take nothing personally, make no assumptions, always do your best—creates opportunity and reduces struggle.

Schneider, Bruce D. *Energy Leadership: Transforming Your Workplace and Your Life from the Core.* Hoboken: John Wiley & Sons, Inc., 2008.

Our thoughts are creative, as our lives demonstrate. Shows how new thoughts and increased, higher energy can improve a dysfunctional work environment. Presents the concept of seven levels of energy, offers ways to become aware of them and move through them toward desired results.

Tolle, Eckhart. *A New Earth: Awakening to Your Life's Purpose*. New York: Plume, 2006.
Being present and becoming more conscious fosters a more meaningful life. The author examines the causes of and reasons for most people's unconsciousness and offers methods to circumvent such conditioning and awaken to the joy within.

ACKNOWLEDGMENTS

I would like to thank Tina Metzger and Ruth Parker for their support during the early stages of this book, and for their "fresh eyes" during the latter.

I would also like to thank Sharlene Cooke for creating the centering exercises. She is truly a beautiful spirit with the ability to help others tap into theirs.

I am very grateful to my creative writing teachers, Doug Jones, who provided a safe place for me to find my voice, and Deirdra McAfee, who encouraged this book forward.

And, for His inspiration and grace, I thank God.

CONTRIBUTING WRITER – CENTERING EXERCISES

Sharlene Cooke is a well-being coach, yoga instructor, and speaker. She suffered from chronic allergies at a young age and noticed her symptoms worsening after she ate certain foods. This sparked in her a fascination with nutrition and natural remedies. To help others improve their health, Cooke offers workshops that focus on healing the body holistically and incorporate mindfulness, nutrition, and yoga. She also offers coaching packages that promote well-being.

In addition to receiving certification as a Nutrition and Wellness Consultant from American Fitness Professionals and Associates, Cooke earned her Certified Professional Coach and Energy Leadership Master Practitioner certifications from the Institute for Professional Excellence in Coaching (iPEC). Cooke is currently completing studies in Ayurveda.

Contact Information for Sharlene Cooke, the Well-Being Life Coach, Sharlene@sharlenecooke.com

ABOUT THE AUTHOR

Patricia C. Brooks, founder of The Courage Catalyst, is an experienced trainer and facilitator and a certified life coach. Through her organization, The Courage Catalyst, she offers highly successful corporate seminars that tackle such topics as enhancing corporate culture, increasing employee engagement, and improving personal effectiveness. She also works directly with organizations and individuals to craft vision statements, develop mission and project plans, and map out effective, timely action toward goals. Her approach, clear and compassionate, individualized and engaging, inspires participants with the confidence to nurture bold, focused, and productive action.

Brooks, who received her MBA from The College of William and Mary, graduated from Mount Holyoke College with a degree in economics. In addition to receiving certification from the Institute of Professional Excellence in Coaching, Brooks has significant project management experience with Fortune 500 corporations; she has been certified as a Project Management Professional for more than a decade.

To book Patricia Brooks for Speaking or Coaching call or email
(804) 304-3768
patricia@thecouragecatalyst.com
www.thecouragecatalyst.com

Made in the USA
Lexington, KY
31 December 2016